This book should be returned to any branch of the
Lancashire County Library on or before the date

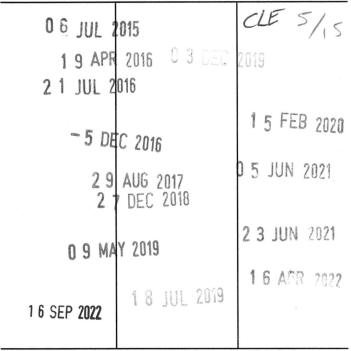

Lancashire County Library
Bowran Street
Preston PR1 2UX

Lancashire
County Council

www.lancashire.gov.uk/libraries

BEN REYNOLDS

CALL ME
CORP

CONTENTS

FOREWORD

This amazing autobiography encapsulates a period of my father, Ben Reynolds' experiences as a soldier in the desert in North Africa and as a prisoner of war in Italy during the Second World War. It is a candid portrait of survival and survivors.

It is written with heart-warming honesty and wit. It shows Ben's courage and initiative under extraordinary pressure and unbearable hardship, and his non-defeatist approach to escape.

His style of writing is so matter of fact that it seems all the more shocking and even ludicrous at times, especially as it is in direct contrast to the way in which we live our lives today.

Call me Corp is an insight into a rarely seen side of human nature. This autobiography is a behavioural study written with disarming humour as Ben searches in his own way to survive.

Having been captured in spectacular fashion by the German Afrika Korps in North Africa, Ben is shipped off to a POW camp in Italy. Experiencing horrific conditions, his words, "We were treated like animals so had no alternative but to act the same," brought tears to his eyes, but did not deter him in his quest to survive.

18 months later, and with great ingenuity, he finally managed to escape and spent a total of 58 days trekking through the Italian countryside. He is captured as a spy and sentenced to death. Ben is taken away to be shot. The nail biting finish combines courage, intelligence and a great deal of faith.

4

Ben's subsequent recognition in the United Kingdom means that he is received at Buckingham Palace by King George VI who presents him with the high honour of the Military Medal, for bravery and courage in the field. His spirit of determination and inventiveness was rewarded.

DEDICATION

Just before my wedding to Chas Hyde in January 1977, I received a note from Dad telling me that a special wedding present was on its way to me in Sydney. Mum and Dad were still living in England. They immigrated to Australia in 1989. Dad said that it would be waiting for me at the Post Office and I would need to sign for it. What could it be? It was obviously something of value.

Later I shared the emotional suspense of opening the small brown parcel in front of Chas. Inside, very carefully wrapped, I found a silver medal mounted on a long silver chain. On one side was the image of King George VI and on the other, the words "For Bravery in the Field". Around the edge of the medal was inscribed 6012060 Sgt. E.F. Reynolds S. Wales Bord. It was his Military Medal.

I knew as soon as I saw the medal on the chain that this was probably going to be the best present my father would ever give me. What marked one of his proudest moments in life was gifted to me. I believe the gift signified his approval. He was happy for me and this was his way of showing it.

I wore his medal on my wedding day, and I have been proud to wear it many times since. Contributing to the presentation and publication of this book has been an absolute pleasure for me. Dad would have been thrilled.

This is Dad's story.

Ben Reynolds' MM - Military Medal 'For bravery in the field'.

A BIT ABOUT BEN

Ernest Frederick (Ben) Reynolds was born on March 1, 1920, in Mistley, Essex, England and died an Australian citizen on August 14, 2004 in Sydney, Australia. He was the youngest of three children born to Priscilla and Arthur Reynolds, Chief Petty Officer, First World War, Second World War.

He'd had a simple education and by 16 years old Ben was a volunteer with the Territorial Army and had begun his training as a carpenter. On September 2, 1939, the day before war was officially declared, Ben was embodied into the army to fight in the Second World War.

Ben was both courageous and inventive and much of his success came from being self-taught and, later, from having the most wonderfully supportive companion in his wife, Ena.

But as children, do we really know our parents?

Two things come to mind when I think of Dad. Firstly, I once asked him what was the most important thing in his life. I didn't mean family, I meant what personally mattered to him, and he replied, "My freedom." And secondly it is his character, as a young man in wartime, portrayed in his memoir *Call me Corp*. In this colourful story, he writes of his escapes from capture. Not always able to trust others, he escaped alone in two desperate attempts to achieve freedom.

My Dad wrote his story down. He wasn't an egotist, far from it. He wrote it to help him, as the family doctor had suggested,

"To get it off your chest," so that he might enjoy a good night's sleep. But it didn't solve his problems. Until he died, he always had to sleep in a separate bed from my mother because he would thrash around. He often ended up on the floor and he told me that he was frightened he might hurt her.

So does this story tell it all? Probably not. It's hard to imagine how great his depth of pain and fear must have been. He represents so many who have endured the conflict of war and who continue to carry it with them.

Ben in uniform, Corporal South Wales Borderers, with his sister Isabelle (inset left) and girlfriend, Ena– later to become his wife.

THE SITUATION

....

The Second World War:
September 3, 1939–August 14, 1945

The beginning of the Second World War was marked by Nazi Germany's invasion of Poland. It was the first step for dictator, Adolf Hitler, in his desire for total supremacy.

Initially, Hitler concentrated his efforts on Germany's neighbours in Europe, but to achieve his goals, there was also the need to control Nort and humiliating defeats at the hands of the British and Commonwealth forces.

For Australians, the first major land battle in the War was in Libya when men of the 6th Division and other Allied troops engaged Italian forces at the town of Bardia, on the coast of Libya. Between 3–5 January 1941, the Italian positions were attacked and Bardia was captured. Over 40,000 Italians were taken prisoner.

The Italians' somewhat ignoble defeat pushed Hitler to send a small force, under the command of General Erwin Rommel, to North Africa to assist them.

From the beginning of 1941, Rommel and his Deutsches Afrika Korps were engaged in many bitter battles with the Allies. And although the Afrika Korps were 'the enemy', the British grew to respect Rommel's ingenuity and wily ways, and the strict discipline of the soldiers who served under his command. He was a leader who would fight alongside his men and the Afrika Korps gave Rommel their loyalty in return.

Subsequently, Rommel became known as 'The Desert Fox'. Capturing the strategically vital Libyan port of Tobruk, on the Mediterranean Sea, was a priority to General Erwin Rommel. It was one of the very few safe ports for supply and transportation and its capture by the Axis armour would disable the Allies. It became a cause for numerous battles.

By December 1941, Tobruk had been under siege for 241 days. The Allies, including a large contingent of Australians, had held out. Not deterred by the long, arduous and monotonous fighting, the Allies had earned an extraordinary reputation, described on Berlin radio as being like, "Poor desert rats caught in a trap." The analogy being that the Allies, like rats, were holed up in Tobruk, and when opportunities arose they would counterattack by sneaking out from their tunnels and hideouts at night to do as much damage as they could, even snatching their enemy's weapons and equipment. Subsequently, a negative, sardonic reference made by the Germans was turned into a positive term with a catch phrase. Thus, the Australians successfully adopted the name, 'The Rats of Tobruk'. With tongue in cheek, 'The Rats of Tobruk' also reflected their famous mate-ship and tenacious resolve.

THE BATTLE OF
GAZALA

....

Where Ben's story begins

In April 1942, the Allied forces of the Eighth Army were commanded by Lieutenant-General Neil Ritchie, under the close supervision of the Commander-in-Chief Middle East, General Sir Claude Auchinleck.

To block the Axis troops and to protect Tobruk, the British had built up a fortified line west of Tobruk. It ran 40 miles south from Gazala, on the Mediterranean coast, and comprised an extensive minefield and fortified 'boxes' of heavily armoured fortresses.

On May 26th, Rommel sent a decoy of men to the Libyan coast and then drove the majority of his troops down and round to the rear of the British forces and the Gazala Line. Simply put, his plan was to take the Allies by surprise, bail them up and then push forward to Tobruk. However, the Allied forces resisted and Rommel had to pull back to a position abutting the British minefield and the heavily armed British, Free French, and Commonwealth troop positions. With his supplies cut off Rommel was subsequently caught in a predicament—though he had the armaments, he did not have the fuel. In this defensive and vulnerable position, Rommel appeared stuck in 'The Cauldron'.

The British and Commonwealth troops had laid mines to block the Axis armour, so German sappers worked to clear a path through the minefield. If they succeeded, Rommel would have a clear line for supply with the Italian forces supporting him.

Map of North Africa

In this vulnerable position, following attack and counterattack, Rommel continued his assaults eventually taking the major French position at Bir Hacheim. Rommel had tipped the scales, the Allies were off balance and between June 11–13 Rommel proceeded to attack the significant British supply bases of Knightsbridge and El Adem until they capitulated. On June 14, the decision was made that the British and Commonwealth soldiers should retreat from the Gazala Line.

General Erwin Rommel discusses tactics with his officers.
Credit: Bundesarchiv, Bild 101I-786-0327-19/Otto/CC-BY-SA.

Ben was captured on June 18th and it was during this time that his story begins.

The Afrika Korps was then able to push forward, capturing Tobruk on June 21st, 1942. Rommel was promoted to the rank of Field Marshal.

On the Battle of Gazala and the subsequent taking of Tobruk by Axis forces, Winston Churchill declared:

"This was one of the heaviest blows I can recall during the war. Not only were its military effects grievous, but it had affected the reputation of the British armies."

Knighted in 1953, Sir Winston Churchill (1874-1965) was the British Prime Minister and statesman who led the country to victory against Nazi Germany and the Axis powers in the Second World War.

Chapter 1

CAIRO OR CAPTURE

....

It was a clear, cold June night in 1942, somewhere outside the perimeter of Tobruk in Northern Libya. I say somewhere, because in those days, the other ranks of the British Army were never really told where they were actually situated. To coin an army expression, "We were never in the picture."

The dugout in which I was sitting with two of my buddies was built up with cases of canned peaches and pears. This was because the position which had been chosen for us consisted of about three feet of sand over solid rock, so to get extra height we had to raid the nearest supply hut and knock off cases of preserved food to surround the dugout.

In our previous position, the dugout had already been built and contained cases of corned beef. It doesn't need much imagination to realise the effect of 120°F on a tin of corned beef when opened. This was just one little problem about the desert. Food generally was plentiful, but water was rationed, so the more experienced soldier always nicked tinned fruit, which allowed him to drink the juice and throw away the solids.

Our dugout was not on stand-by duty this night, which

meant we could sleep. I was sitting at one end with an overcoat and blanket slung around me, as I was cold. I wished I was in the comfort of Cairo where I'd had 14 days leave two months previous.

Over the top peered our platoon officer.

"Wake up you chaps," he said.

"Sir!" I replied.

"Get your men out of that flea-pit and follow me."

"Yes, Sir," I replied.

Only too pleased to have a walk around, I looked at my watch and saw it was 1.30 a.m.

We were about 20-strong and sat in a disorganised heap. Our officer, who was new to our battalion, had just opened his mouth, and with the authority bestowed upon him at the age of 19 years by some UK officer training establishment, said, "Now you men, quietness is essential."

Then there was an almighty yell. Smudge had sat on a scorpion. Well if anybody had let off a mighty fart it could not have caused more laughter, which of course meant noise. 15 minutes later, after Smudge had been carted off by medical stretcher-bearers (which, by the way, was the last I ever saw of him), our platoon officer continued, "We are to withdraw this position within the next one and a half hours."

According to him we were completely surrounded by Germans. Better still, to quote him, "A complete Panzer Division."

Whether or not he was trying to frighten us into alertness I wasn't sure. I was to find that out later. But at the time, I just felt like crawling back into my dugout.

We were to march in fours, following as closely as possible to those in front, because we would be passing through various minefields of our own. I hoped for this reason that the officers might know where the mines actually were, but I had my doubts, even though the mines belonged to us.

"No need to carry ammunition, travel as light as possible, five rounds at the most," we were told.

But we didn't bother about ammunition at all. What good would five rounds be, if we met trouble? And if our platoon officer said a Panzer Division was behind us, it seemed quite ridiculous.

After considerable chaos, for it was very dark, we moved off in a direction unknown, or as far as I was concerned, unknown. The going wasn't difficult; it was cold, and walking wasn't

German Panzer Mk IIIs on the move in the desert.
Credit: Bundesarchiv, Bild 101I-783-0109-11 / Dörner / CC-BY-SA.

unpleasant. It was never a march, and it all proved uneventful.

We arrived at what was obviously the main Tobruk road and in the half-light of dawn; one could distinguish a line of trucks—some already loaded with troops from other units. Nobody, but nobody, seemed to know what was happening. It seemed to me that at a time like this, the best thing to do was to sit down. Then after a while, lie down, and if a senior NCO (non-commissioned officer) or officer happened to attack you with words the like of which you'd not heard since your old man stood on a nail, then you'd tell him you didn't feel so good, and at the same time, look as if you were about to throw up all over the place. He'd soon depart with a grunt like, "There's a lot to do."

This time I didn't get abused, but it might initially have been better if I had, although as it turned out later, it would not have altered my eventual fate.

Of all things, I went to sleep. When I awoke, I found my two buddies, and five others whom I'd seen around (but didn't really know) lying close by.

Our battalion had gone!

I can assure you I had little idea what to do. There were a few military police and a number of empty trucks standing off the road and the sun was warming up. I just couldn't believe so much movement could have taken place and I had slept through it. I bawled out the seven others who were with me for not waking me up, as to bawl was the right thing to do if you had a couple of stripes.

"Not our fault," said one of them, "We were asleep as well."

I threatened him with a 252, which is an army charge sheet. When this was made out and handed into Company headquarters, it allowed you the next morning to have the accused marched in before the Company commander for him to be reckoned with. However, as this was quite impossible in the present situation, it seemed rather ridiculous to me, but it did have the right effect.

We walked a hundred yards or so to the road when up came an enquiring military police sergeant on his motorcycle.

"What are you lot doing?" he asked.

I felt like saying, "Going for a bunk-up in Cairo," But thought better of it. Instead I said, "We've been on a rear guard

EAST ANGLIAN TANK MEN IN DESERT: Ex-Police-constable A. R. Portway, formerly of the Colchester Borough Police, and Mrs. Portway, now of the Hare and Hounds, East Bergholt, received on Thursday this photograph of local men then serving in the Royal Tank Regiment in the Middle East. Driver Jack Portway (seated on the right) is their son; centre (seated) is a sergeant from West Mersea; and on the left is Corpl. Reynolds (Manningtree). Standing, on the right, is a Colchester man named Jones.

On leave in Cairo—Ben (left bottom row) and members of his unit.

21

and the battalion has left us behind to destroy radio equipment. After which we were supposed to meet them, and travel by truck to a transit camp in Heliopolis, situated outside Cairo… but they seem to have gone."

"You can take one of those trucks and follow that road," he suggested.

"Well," I thought, "We might just as well go to Cairo, as anywhere else."

If I was wrong about Cairo I felt it would be an understandable mistake, especially when you didn't know where you were supposed to be going in the first place.

By this time, we had more or less forgotten that we had been cut off by a Panzer Division, and that was if our platoon officer was to be believed. So, why let a small thing like that worry us? We would go to Cairo.

I gave the order to load jerry cans of petrol from the other trucks into the main truck, which I thought had taken the least hammering during its tour of active service. About 15 cans of petrol and various saleable objects were loaded aboard.

Every soldier that I knew in the desert could drive a truck, for apart from going into a sand dune; there wasn't much else you could hit—not where I had been anyway. However, it turned out that we had a professional driver amongst us, so that quickly settled any discussion about who was to drive.

To the uninitiated, it might have seemed strange that trucks should just stand around waiting to be taken, but under circumstances such as a withdrawal it would not be uncommon. We moved off, and by my best-captured German watch the time was 8.10 a.m. Cairo, here we come—to look for our unit of course!

Chapter 2

CAPTURED!

....

We had been travelling for just over an hour, when we realised that we had only one and a half bottles of water between us. Still, we were not too concerned because we would meet somebody, somewhere along the route—and we did in the next ten minutes. But it wasn't what we were expecting.

To my horror, the road was blocked by a line of blazing trucks and bewildered soldiers, who were walking around and sitting about not knowing what to do. I enquired as to what the hell had happened. Apparently, Jerry had attacked them from the air with two aircraft, which had happened only five minutes prior to our arrival.

Up came a junior officer to enquire what we were about and to my horror he said, "Get out! We are taking over your truck."

As you may be aware, a lot of things can travel through one's mind in a very short period of time and I thought of many things to try and put him off the idea, but none seemed plausible enough. Cairo seemed suddenly so much further away.

Jerry settled everything for us quite nicely.

Wham! Out of the sun came a German fighter aircraft,

straight at us, machine guns blazing. Even more to my surprise, immediately on his tail was a Kitty Hawk, trying to overload the Hun with lead. You might well think, "Why sit around in a truck while all this is happening?" Well, so did I.

My first reaction to the event was to move my arse on the seat as I thought I'd shat myself. The shock had pumped right through me. I hadn't but our driver had, poor bastard, and understandably so, for he'd been shot in the leg. I shouted through to the back of the truck for another driver to take over. We had no time to help the first one out and into the back, so we moved him between us, which must have been miserable for him to say the least. But I felt he still had a chance of arriving in Cairo if he didn't bleed to death.

I knew if we turned left, we would hit the sea. That wouldn't be so good. On the other hand, if we turned right, we would go into the desert, even maybe get lost, but that wouldn't be such a bad thing at a time like this.

Jerry had turned, coming in for another run, and was still being followed by the Kitty Hawk. Jerry seemed to treat the Hawk with contempt. I couldn't help laughing with horror at how vulnerable we were and how unbelievable it all seemed for behind the Kitty Hawk was a second Jerry. How long that skirmish went on, we didn't stay to find out. With the driver's foot flat to the floor into the blue we went.

Ten minutes or so had passed. "Which way, Corp?" asked the driver.

"Straight on," I said. I thought that was the best thing to say.

When you were trained as a wartime soldier, you were taught how to use a rifle, a light machine gun and a bayonet; to put in a frontal attack on a copse or hill, how to clean buttons and cap badges to mirror brightness and toe caps of boots the same. To march, swinging your arms in unison, how to stay alert on guard duty and turn out the guard in ten seconds flat when commanded to do so; but never what to do if you were in the desert on your own, with the enemy all around you.

Then I remembered that I had an army issue compass in my haversack. This I had 'acquired' at some time or other, for you were never issued with such an item under the rank of sergeant. I can recall having a lecture on the prismatic compass during my Territorial Army days and this helped to serve me well.

Now, "straight on" to my driver meant the same as "straight on" to a sidewinder snake, although you couldn't really blame him. Being in the desert had one advantage, there was nothing to hit. But with no discernable point as a focus, straight on in the desert, if you didn't take note of the sun, would be the same as being at sea in a thick fog without a compass.

I felt very frustrated, "Where the bloody hell is the sun?" I asked.

"Don't know Corp, must be up there somewhere."

Looking at my compass, I discovered that we were travelling west—back to more or less from where we had come.

"Turn the truck around until I say straight on," I said.

"Which way? He asked, "Left or right?"

"Any bloody way," I snapped.

For the first time and from that moment on I felt I really had some responsibility. It was a strange feeling, as if my life had altered. Swinging the truck round, the compass showed due east. I knew we were west of Sallum Pass, close to the Egyptian border, and felt we must try for this.

Groans were coming from our wounded driver, although he was fully conscious.

"How are you, Jim?" I asked.

"Alright Corp," he replied.

"Can we stop, Corp?" he asked.

"What for?"

"I need a shit."

"Too late, mate, double deck it. You did that nearly an hour ago and from the look of your leg and the blood on the floor, I can understand it." I turned and smiled to him.

He returned a faint smile and passed out. I would have stopped the truck to try and help him, but there was nothing I could do. His leg was badly smashed.

We were bouncing around all over the place. It was a rough ride. Cairo was at least another four or five hundred miles away—or that's what I thought. The sun was up and it was hell. The unlined roof of the cab acted as an oven. I looked at him and felt he couldn't survive much longer and wondered what to do with him when he died. I told the driver to stop. We carried Jim into the back of the truck, and laid him on the floor.

"Give me a handkerchief," I requested of the other six, and would you believe it, we didn't have one between us.

One of them tore the sleeve out of his mate's shirt. This I soaked in water and lay over Jim's head. He didn't stir.

"Don't let him roll about," I said, "Look after him."

The canvas hood over the back of the truck would be considerably cooler than the roof of the cab.

We moved off again and way ahead was an escarpment. I had only just noticed it when my head suddenly felt as if it were on fire, with a million bells ringing; I felt I was going to pass out with dizziness. My driver brought me out of it with a yell. "Bloody hell!"

The back of his left hand was a mass of raw flesh with finger stumps sticking out. I couldn't believe my eyes. It seemed a lifetime before I could pull myself together and realise we were under fire.

"Flat out!" I yelled.

"What about the springs?" He said. "If we break them we will never get to Cairo."

"Bugger the springs, flat out!" I replied.

And 'flat out' he went, straight over the steering wheel! He had passed out.

I turned off the ignition and the vehicle came to a stop. To put it bluntly I didn't know whether my asshole was bored or punctured, or what to do. There was pandemonium in the back. One had been shot dead and the remainder were feeling somewhat afraid and confused to say the least. I climbed out of the cab, walked to the back of the truck and told them not to worry. I don't know why, because whoever was out there, Jerry or Wop (Italian) was still firing.

"Climb down one at a time and lay down by the side of the truck." I pointed to the side protected from the firing.

There were four of them. Our present count: two wounded, one dead and five of us to go. I noticed one chap had brought his rifle with him.

"Bury that in front of you now, and don't let a bit of it show, unless you want the lot of us shot." I ordered. Now this must have been sheer instinct. I remembered when I was a lad of ten years, my parents bought me a pair of boxing gloves for Christmas. Feeling a type of one-upmanship, I took my new gloves to the gymnasium the following Tuesday, where I was a member of the gymnastics display team, and I showed them about. Another member, from the boxing group, produced another pair of gloves from a cupboard, which he proceeded to pull on.

"Put yours on. We will try them out," he said.

I did and got the hiding of my life. Was there a comparison?

The enemy shooting at us, who must arrive eventually, will see the rifle even with no ammunition, and 'Bang! Bang!' All

dead. We could clearly hear the machine gun crack away—
though as yet couldn't see it, it was coming our way. I felt
there was only one thing to do—surrender—something else we
had never been told about.

Why I didn't think of waving something, even if it wasn't
white, I don't know. I turned to the four lying beside me,
"Sorry about this fellas, but we've had it." I walked out away
from the truck, with my hands stretched as high as possible
above my head. I carried on a good 30 feet clear of the
truck, hoping and repeating the silent prayer that I would be
clearly seen. Although it seemed an age, the firing stopped. I
breathed again.

From nowhere, surrounded by a cloud of dust, a German
army armoured vehicle appeared. It stopped about 50 yards
in front of me. I didn't move. My eyes were transfixed on the
snout of the machine gun pointing straight at me. I thought it
better to let him make the next move, which again seemed
an age. He moved gently towards me and stopped suddenly at
25 yards, as if suspicious. I wondered if he had guessed that
my men were lying behind the truck and if so, he was wondering
what armament they had. I felt I had to do something quickly
in case they became too touchy and opened up.

"Get up, one at a time," I shouted to my chaps. "Put your
hands up as high as you can, and walk towards me, and don't
dig up that rifle!"

It took no more than two or three minutes for this
manoeuvre to be completed. One whimpered a little, "He's
going to shoot us down."

"Shut up!" I ordered. "And keep your trap shut."

For this was the only language some could understand.

Now I ordered them to walk forward. "When I say 'far
enough' make sure you stop."

We walked about 15 paces towards the armoured vehicle. I ordered them to stop. We were now within 30 feet. Your move next, I thought.

After what seemed another age, but was possibly only seconds, a young German officer climbed out of the vehicle, and with Luger pistol in hand he walked towards us. I noticed he walked to one side, allowing his machine gunner to have a

Soldier with dust mask. Goggles and face covering are worn to protect against the many sand storms.
Credit: Bundesarchiv, Bild 101I-785-0285-14A/Otto/CC-BY-SA

clear field of view. I murmured to my chaps not to lower their hands until instructed. The officer walked to within six feet of us, caked with dust, and when he lifted up his goggles, large, white circles showed around his eyes.

He now had a backup—a German NCO beside him with a light automatic weapon. He must have noticed the two stripes on my shirtsleeve and beckoned me forward with a motion of his finger. I hesitated, in case I had misunderstood him. He repeated the movement with a verbal order. He spoke in English, "Come here, Corporal!"

I walked forward and stopped in front of him. I felt my hands stretched high was a bit stupid at this stage, but refrained from lowering them.

"Come with me," he said.

We walked a few paces on and stopped. He turned towards me, his Luger still directed towards my stomach.

"You're a lucky man, Tommy!" he said.

"You're right," I thought, especially when he took from my hand my steel helmet. Right through it was a neat hole in the back and at the front. It was a large hole, with the metal turned back in strips. He placed his finger against the leather headband, which had been severed by a bullet. It must have passed through the helmet, at the same time as my driver had been shot in the back of the hand. It was difficult to believe what I saw. Nobody could be that lucky, but that's how it goes.

"Where have you come from?" he asked. "And lower your hands."

Now, I thought, diplomacy is important. If I tell him I'm not sure, he will shoot me, or at least kick me, and I couldn't pause to think up something for he would think I was making it up.

"I was in a convoy, Sir, on the Tobruk road and we were shot up by your aircraft. I managed to get away."

"Where were you going?" he asked.

"I think to Tobruk, Sir."

"Why that way when all your troops are going in the opposite direction?"

"Orders, Sir, follow the crowd."

He looked a little bewildered.

"You will march your men towards the escarpment. We will be right behind you."

"But Sir, I have one dead and two wounded in the truck, one of whom is in a bad way. Can we not drive the truck?"

He sent his sergeant over to the truck to inspect. Words were passed to and fro in German, which I didn't understand.

"OK Tommy! March on! We will take care of them later."

We had not been walking for more than five minutes when a German truck came alongside. A few brisk words were exchanged between the driver and our officer. We were then loaded into the truck and the armoured vehicle moved off; believe it or not, the officer gave us a short wave of the hand and a big smile.

Within a few minutes, we were over the escarpment and ordered out of the truck. I could not believe my eyes. There, sitting in a heap on the ground were literally hundreds of captured Allied soldiers: UK, Indians, South Africans, Free French and Allied vehicles parked all around.

We were ushered amongst the others and told to sit. The first thing we were asked by those who were already taken prisoner was if we had any water. It was then that I realised that I had left mine on the truck. From then on I really felt thirsty.

Germans with light automatic weapons were positioned in a circle around us. It was organised chaos for the Germans, and defeat and complete bewilderment for us.

During the rest of the day, low-flying fighters came

overhead, low enough to see the pilot clearly.

If it was a German, an officer would send up a red flare.

If it was a British aircraft, he would send up a white.

The aircraft would make two runs. It appeared as if they were looking on the first run, and on the second they would see the flare and fly off. It was a tense moment for prisoner and captors. We were all sitting ducks for any aircraft.

I thought to myself, the Kitty Hawks would be brought back, an attack would be made and we would be rescued. But they must have had more pressing things to do.

As the day passed on, at least 100 more prisoners joined us.

One British truck, with some Indian Sikhs aboard, unknowingly drove straight into the position. When they realised what it was all about, particularly when Jerry opened up on them with machine guns, they stopped immediately, and to be fair, so did the German firing.

The German Afrika Korps were really quite a decent lot.

The Sikhs climbed out of the truck, obviously very frightened and stunned. One had a rifle in his hand but obviously had no intention of using it. I saw him keel over as he was shot with a single bullet from one of the guards. It was understandable; they could not have taken a chance on his using it.

During the day, I noticed our truck was brought in. By this time I was feeling thirstier.

One of the chaps who was with me from the beginning said they hadn't brought Jim and the others out of the truck. I never did find out what happened. It was possible that an ambulance could have taken them away as I hadn't noticed any wounded amongst us. My main interest was the half-bottle of water that I'd left hanging in the cab, and the cartons of Cape to Cairo cigarettes in the back. These would have financed our trip to Cairo.

Chapter 3

NO GOING HOME

Darkness came, night passed, and it was so cold I shall never forget it. All I was wearing was a shirt and shorts. Dawn broke, the sun came up, and warmth once more came into my body. But then it was the reverse— it was so hot it was difficult to breathe.

We were suffering from thirst. Although some hadn't eaten for 36 hours, it meant nothing, for thirst was the most demanding thing to satisfy.

It was around 10 a.m. I say 'around', because I had hidden my watch in my stocking; the German troopers would have identified it as one of theirs, if it were discovered. That would certainly have caused some awkward questions.

I sat with my knees up and my head resting on them, dozing in the heat, trying to forget the dryness of my mouth and the soreness of my lips. The only consolation was that I was not alone.

I looked up, and there standing in front of me surveying the prisoners was the German officer who had taken us prisoner. He looked at me and smiled. I realised that he had possibly recognised me by my steel helmet, which was on my head. Wearing it was more by force of habit. I got up slowly and said, "Good morning, Sir, may I ask you a favour?"

He grinned and said, "If you want to go home, no you can't."

"It's easier than that, Sir," I replied.

"Standing over there is my truck. All I want to do is to get to it and get some cigarettes which are in the back."

He half smiled and turned away, at the same time calling to one of the guards who came running to him. He gave the guard what appeared to be a brisk order, then turned to me: "Go with the guard, Tommy. Oh, and by the way, did you understand what I said to him?"

"No Sir," I replied.

"I told him to shoot you if you put one step out of place."

I retrieved three cartons of cigarettes, a jersey and my half bottle of water. My guard took the water from me and tossed it to one side. It then became obvious to me whilst we were half dead from thirst we could be of no danger to our captors. The cigarettes were of little use. It was quite impossible to smoke because my mouth was so dry. But had I kept them they would have been very useful in the future, for they have terrific bargaining power, quite beyond belief.

Rumour went round that we were to get a water ration. How that was going to take place under the present circumstances heaven only knew. It was now about noon and very hot. The Indians were in a very bad way. Water seemed more important to them than anything. They wailed on and on until we felt like shooting them.

"Pane, pane!" they cried which is Urdu for water.

Once more I noticed my friendly German officer talking to a guard. Then, handing the guard a fruit tin, he pointed towards me. The guard came over and gave it to me. I was disappointed. It was empty. He said nothing and walked away. I couldn't understand this move. 20 minutes later, a water wagon drew up about 20 yards in front of us.

All hell broke loose. There was one big rush by the Indians towards the truck and some of the Europeans amongst them. As we were sitting at the outer group of prisoners nearest to the truck, I, and many others in that area, got kicked and trampled on.

My eyes were filled with sand and were sore for two or three days. I could hear a hell of a lot of shooting going on, but in the confusion it was difficult to comprehend what was happening. Within five minutes it was not so difficult to see what had happened. The only way the Germans could hold back the water-mad crowd, was by firing into them. There must have been 30 dead and wounded lying near the truck. I felt no sorrow or pity. I was livid. My pear tin had been flattened and my leg torn by a boot. I picked up the tin and straightened it out as best as I could.

Amongst us we had about a dozen sergeant majors. They were called out for a conference with the Germans. The idea was to sort us into groups, and then take us in single file to the water truck to receive our water. One fruit tin full per man tipped into his steel helmet. I mentally thanked my German officer for the tin he had given me. He knew my helmet had a hole in it. Many drank their ration of water straight down and immediately vomited it up again. It was difficult to control myself and not do exactly the same.

Soon after the water rationing, the guards started separating us into groups of about 100. I was amongst the first batch. This I made sure of as I was a bit fed up with sitting around. I was feeling 'anything for a change'. I was still thirsty, but I was afraid to drink my remaining water.

We were marched off or, rather, we shuffled off for what seemed like a century but could only have been 30 minutes. We were loaded onto three trucks, escorted by an armoured car. Off we went in a cloud of dust, eventually hitting the main road, which I estimated to be west of Tobruk.

We must have been travelling for about four hours when the truck stopped.

To my absolute horror, milling about the back of the truck were a crowd of Italian soldiers looking like death warmed up and behaving as if they had been responsible for capturing us.

This was one thing I dreaded, for it was believed by the British soldier that the 'Iti' were a sorry lot, and no way could they be taken by them. That would be the worst insult of all.

We were unloaded from the trucks and assembled by a camel pond, from where we could drink filthy stagnant, camel-pissy water. It was hot and sweet. I washed my face and hands while some drank, and spewed straight back into the pond. We were reassembled and once more sat in a heap.

A couple of German officers came along and told us that we would be staying here for the night. They apologised for handing us over to the Italian forces, but said they couldn't help it as they had some unfinished business to attend to. We were told the next day our rank, name and number would be taken and passed on to London by the Red Cross.

I drank a drop more of my water and decided to have a cigarette. Of course, I needed a light and darkness this time was falling upon us. I called amongst those present for a light and bartered a carton of Cape to Cairo cigarettes for a box of matches. I took two or three drags of the weed and stubbed it out wishing I had never lit it. My mouth seemed to seize up. It had not properly recovered from the lack of water. I dumped the rest of the cigarettes and that was my first mistake.

My second mistake was when I pushed a five-foot Wop, who was shoving me around the next morning whilst we were being loaded onto a truck. He swung his rifle round and caught me in the chin and I still carry the mark. I came round later on the truck, feeling like death. My water can and pullover had gone.

Chapter 4

LIKE NOTHING ON EARTH

We moved off by truck to an unknown railhead, where we were loaded into cattle rail trucks, which transported us to what turned out to be Tarhuna. I discovered later that Tarhuna was situated approximately 50 miles southeast of Tripoli. We were unloaded from the train and once more into road trucks. The whole journey of some 500 miles was very distressing to say the least. I cannot recall any similarity in the feeling I had, before or since.

The human body can stand so much before it breaks, and in many cases it did. It was sad to see the expression on some of the chaps' faces.

On boarding the trucks, we were given a small tin of meat the size of a tin of baby food, and one water biscuit about four inches square and at least three quarters of an inch thick, which was as hard as a paving slab, but still no issue of water.

Now, as soon as those with teeth tried to bite into the biscuit, there were shouts of bloody hell and the like. At least it broke the tension and laughter followed. This relieved more tension. But it was pretty obvious that it wasn't happy laughter. Those who did succeed in chewing the biscuit nearly suffocated. The dryness of the mouth and the dryness of the biscuit literally seized up the mouth and throat. It was a frightening experience, for some who had attempted to swallow the dry mass had difficulty in bringing it out again. Their faces were contorted. Naturally I had made no attempt at eating mine. I couldn't, as my jaw was cut, swollen and very sore. Oddly enough, it cheered me up to see others suffering—to share in my pain, if you like.

The trucks pulled up outside a number of sandy coloured buildings. They were ground floor only, quite stark looking, and there appeared to be nothing else there. It certainly didn't look like home.

We were unloaded from our trucks and lined up in ranks of five, with the usual pushing and shoving by our guards. We were then marched towards a large pair of timber gates covered in barbed wire. This was the main entrance to the camp. Over these gates in large writing were the words: 'Campo Concentratione'.

"There appears to be no one in," was the first comment from a bespectacled young man with a very cultured voice.

At the time I thought that was very amusing. I realised again my jaw was sore when I instinctively laughed but it just had to stay sore, especially when a Cockney chirped up, "What did you expect, a Royal welcome?"

The camp was a series of nine sandy coloured buildings, which all had stone tiled floors. The windows were not at the normal height one would expect but very shallow, quite long and positioned at the top of the wall. It turned out that the buildings were originally for fruit storage. The perimeter was surrounded by high barbed wire and thick in depth.

It is difficult to explain the total depression that overwhelmed all of us. We felt totally defeated and completely lost; it was like nothing on earth.

We were counted off in fifties and allocated a unit. During this time, other trucks were arriving with troops I had not seen before. They had been taken prisoner in other areas.

By the middle of the afternoon things began to happen.

Into the building came three guards brandishing their rifles and ordering us outside. The only word of English they seemingly knew was 'Outside'. If they had listened and paid attention (as they should have done) they would have learnt another: 'Bollocks'. For that was the reply they normally got, although we complied with their instructions reasonably smartly. It would otherwise have meant a bang round the head with a rifle butt.

We were formed up in rows of five, ten deep. This took a fair time because of the language barrier. At this time there were about 200 of us.

A British RSM (Regimental Sergeant Major) was put in charge of us and was responsible for us to our captors. There seemed to be a lot of hurrying here and there by the guards and an awful lot of shouting.

Something was obviously going to happen.

Then it did. A bugle blasted out, creating more tension from the guards. In through the gate came the person we would know from that day on as our Camp Commandant.

It was indeed one of those sights that embedded itself in your memory for life.

He was about five feet tall, weighing around 13 stone and dressed in a uniform of pale blue riding britches and black leather riding boots. He also wore a black Sam Brown-type belt, forage cap and held a riding crop. His chest was emblazoned with dozens of medals. Held firmly between his lips was a twin cigarette holder with two cigarettes alight. He was escorted by two junior officers and a corporal; the latter turned out to be the interpreter.

I felt sorry for this tired-looking corporal for he was old. My reason for being sorry was that he looked so poorly dressed. Scruffy clothes, baggy trousers, and his boots were worn right

Camp commandant and interpreter.
"He did more for our morale than he realised. He was the topic of conversation for days after."

down at the heels. To cap it all, he looked very frightened.

The party stopped in front of us. A large box the size of a tea chest was then placed on the ground and the Commandant was helped up onto it. This was terrible for my jaw as no one could stop laughing. He did more for our morale than he realised. He was the topic of conversation for days after.

He stood on his box, pushing out his chest and removing the cigarette holder at the same time. He then straightened his forage cap and, slapping the side of his boot with his riding crop, he looked down at one of his juniors and snapped out an order in Italian. He wanted his interpreter closer to him. The Commandant addressed us in a loud screaming voice. Why he found it necessary to shout so much I don't know because none of us could understand him. The translation came from beside him:

"The Commandant says you will keep quiet and listen."
The interpreter was using a horn as used by a rowing Cox.
"The Commandant says you are Prisoners of War of the Italian people. You will do as you are told or be shot."

Now you will always find, amongst a gathering of 200 people such as ours, one with a sense of humour; always ready to dice against the odds, and yes *we* had one. During the pause of translation he sent out a mighty raspberry.

The Commandant's face changed from a pale pasty colour to brilliant red. He screamed and shouted. The guards dashed here and there trying to look as if they were doing their best to find the culprit. Then the interpreter translated: "The Commandant says you will get no food today. This is your punishment."

Then damn me if the culprit didn't let off another raspberry. The Commandant stumbled off his box with all hands helping him, and you would never have heard such a stream of shouting and screaming again if you lived to 100 years. He stomped out of the camp with his riding crop thrashing against his leg. He even took a swing at the poor old interpreter. We were then counted and returned to our buildings.

I am quite sure that we would not have got any food that day, not hot food anyway, for on discovering the kitchens we found they were open fronted, with stone top work tables and wood fires which were out. Apart from this there were no cooking utensils, no wood for the fires and certainly no cook.

Evening was coming on and it would soon be dark. It was then that we all realised that we had nothing to sleep on, nor blankets to cover ourselves. It looked as if it was to be a long cold night. It proved to be impossible to lie down for any length of time. The stone floor was so cold. So, we sat leaning against the wall all night. We also realised that we didn't know where the toilets were. We just had to hang it outside the door, as we had instructions that if we left the building after dark we would be shot.

Chapter 5

CAMPO CONCENTRATIONE

Daylight came at last, which was welcomed by all, and into the buildings came the guards shouting, "Out, out!" This would be a pleasure. We were counted and then sent back to our building once more. Feeling somewhat bewildered I thought that it simply couldn't continue for much longer. We hadn't seen hot food for what seemed like years. Now that we were getting ample water and the thirst had been well quenched, one realised that one hadn't eaten for a very long time.

Two hours later we were asked to fall in for our RSM. This we did with keenness for it meant information. The mind needed to know what was happening. The RSM was accompanied by an Italian junior officer who spoke a little English and was much more pleasant than our crotchety old Camp Commandant.

It appeared that we were to have a sergeant in charge of each block and the RSM in overall charge. Food would be issued once daily. We were to draw from stores: one straw palliasse which turned out to be drastically short of straw, one Italian-style Billy can, one metal drinking mug and one spoon. We were told that if we lost them there would be no more issued. Knives were taboo. We were also informed that, as this was not a proper Prisoner of War (POW) Camp, we would not be

Reference: Cas/Sect/2..
Infantry Record Office,
EXETER.
16th July, 1942.

To:- Mrs. P. Reynolds,
"Midge",
Colchester Road,
Lawford, Essex.

Sir or Madam,
I have to inform you that your son 's name - No. 6012060 Corporal E.F. REYNOLDS, The South Wales Borderers - appears in a list of British soldiers, broadcast from foreign wireless stations and picked up in this Country, in which it is stated that the soldier was captured in the recent fighting in Africa and is now a Prisoner of War.
I am also to state that, whilst there is no reason to doubt he is a Prisoner of War, he must remain posted as "Missing" pending the receipt of an Official Prisoner of War report.
I am,
Sir or Madam,
Your obedient Servant,

Lieut-Colonel
for Lieut-Colonel, Officer i/c
Infantry Record Office.

CWC/RW.

July 1942: Ben's mother received comfort in knowing that Ben had not been killed.

allowed to write letters and there would be no issue of Red Cross parcels. These privileges would be forthcoming when we arrived in Italy and no one knew when that would be.

The food—which was to be issued daily—would be cooked by our own cooks. Each Group Sergeant, along with two men, would collect the bulk ration for each building daily at 12 noon. This seemed to boost the morale of all concerned.

Just think, 'cooked food'.

Two cooks with experience were chosen. They would be given three fatigue men to help with chores. Payment for this chore would be half a cup of soup extra and for the cooks, one cup. Our meal for this day would be at 3 p.m. and after that 12 noon. We just couldn't wait.

BROOKS (MISTLEY) LTD.,
MISTLEY,
MANNINGTREE, ESSEX.
'Phone : MANNINGTREE 37 (3 Lines),
'Gram : BROOKS LTD., MANNINGTREE,

DIRECTORS :
F. V. CRIST   G. A. BROOKS
W. H. BROOKS   C. E. WARD
J. V. BOLTON   G. A. E. NEVILLE
G. S. SARSON

Mrs. Reynolds,
Midge,
Colchester Road,
Lawford.

Date 3-7-42.   Ref   HGD.

Dear Mrs Reynolds,
    Mrs Attfield Brooks has just telephoned to say that quite by chance her Gardener happened to be listening to the German news in English when he heard that a Sergt Reynolds of Colchester Road, Manningtree was a prisoner in their hands.
    We wondered if it might be your son and if so thought we would lose no time in letting you know in case you had a communication from the War Office that he was missing.
    We sincerely hope that the time is not too far distant when the present strife will be brought to a victorious conclusion and all husbands, sons, and relations will be able to resume their normal mode of living.

                                    Yours truly,
                              BROOKS(MISTLEY)LTD.,
                              Asst Secretary

A moving letter to Ben's mother, July 1942.

We were also told that as from now we could walk about the camp compound. But the area of the cookhouse was strictly out of bounds. Also, we were not to approach within six feet of the perimeter fence, which was marked with a single strand of barbed wire.

The Camp Commandant would visit us once a day and everyone would stand still as he approached. Misbehaviour of any sort or rudeness towards the Camp Commandant would mean forfeiture of rations for the whole camp.

We queued for our palliasse, blanket and other supplies, and returned with our spoils to our buildings. I immediately scratched my name on my belongings whilst others messed about trying out their palliasses. This was a real giggle, for if you picked it up from one end the straw, which was pulped up, would just drop to the other end. They were hopeless but better than nothing at all.

"Skilly up!" went the cry and that's how we were called to our food from then on.

'Skilly' is described in the dictionary as a soup or broth as served in prisons and workhouses. What we got was certainly not good enough for that. The rations were diabolical—one mug (less than half a pint) of clear thin soup per day. Twice a week it would have vegetables, such as spinach in it, and once a week small cubes of meat the size of an Oxo cube. This worked out, if you were lucky, one cube per person and what a job it was working that out. If two pieces dropped into your mug you had to hook one piece out with your fingers and put it back. I have seen chaps place the two pieces in the palm of their hand so as to compare size and return the smaller. This sort of thing caused a lot of feeling and an awful lot of shouting from those waiting.

Also once a week, always on a Thursday, a small piece of

Italian cheese would be issued, approximately 15 grams. This, needless to say, always tasted fantastic.

The bread ration daily was 200 grams, about the size of a bread roll and always pudding like and very heavy. The bread ration was God. Some would sell their souls for it; some would barter it, as I did. Some prisoners would make this small portion last until the next ration, or even longer to the extent of hording it.

It would be fascinating to watch them and even annoying at times. They would take it out sometimes up to 20 times a day, and then nibble a little piece off the corner.

Others would lay it on their mattress, stare at it and after an hour have a nibble. Some sat for hours in this manner.

These types I found the worst to suffer. Jealousy would be rife. You would hear such remarks as, "How much bread have you got?"

"Half a loaf." Would be the reply.

"Liar, impossible. Show me." Would be the answer.

Attempts at fighting would break out over this, usually started by the one with the least. This sort of thing would mostly happen amongst friends who had actually served together.

I stayed a loner. I spoke to all but had no close friends, for I was certain that this wasn't a 'here today and gone tomorrow' situation. It was going to be a long haul and would be the survival of the fittest. I could not afford friends.

Chapter 6

SETTING UP
BUSINESS

I had to find something to help improve my conditions. I couldn't think of anything, until one day we received a ration of ten Nationale (Belgian) cigarettes. This was going to be a weekly event, if we all behaved. Now these cigarettes were issued in a soft paper packet, which meant they were not air tight and quickly dried out. This also meant if you were not careful the tobacco would fall out from one end. Consequently, I had the idea of visiting the cook and for the price of one cigarette he would suspend them over his cook pot. The steam would make the tobacco swell. I then had a more presentable product.

The issue of this cigarette ration was rather interesting. Those, such as myself, would smoke the ten in two days. But the bread hoarders were normally non-smokers and would hoard them and watch over them as they would their bread. After a day without a smoke I would be yearning for a fag. I approached one of the hoarders and offered him a third of my bread ration for his ten cigarettes and to my surprise he said, "Yes."

I then placed a firm order with him for his next week's cigarette ration. The following day I gave two thirds of my bread ration, a third each to two other non-smokers, for ten cigarettes from each of them. By the next cigarette ration I owned ten packets—100 cigarettes. I felt really rich.

As far as I was concerned, a third of a loaf was just as good as a whole one especially as I had obtained 20 cigarettes in exchange for the other two thirds. I found smoking staved off my hunger.

Others, however, soon discovered this too—that a loaf could be better than any money, and cigarettes could be purchased. This consequently put up the price. A whole loaf became equal to ten cigarettes. Times were getting hard and I had to think again.

The Italian guards always seemed hard done-by. They were old in comparison to us. They must have been around the 50-year mark. This seemed old as we had an average age of 23 years.

One morning I was sitting near the perimeter wire when one of these guards came strolling by on his usual sentry duty. I smiled. He stopped and put his fingers to his mouth, as if smoking. I realised he couldn't be offering me a cigarette, for what would I have to trade back? It became obvious that he was asking for a smoke. Now, how was I to tell this man that I would be prepared to give him a smoke, but in exchange I would want a pair of scissors and a knife? I tried sign language, which proved useless. How was I going to explain this?

He was furtively looking over his shoulder in case he was

observed. He then mumbled something and moved off. I knew I had a sharp one there and he would be back. Now I had to plan. The scissors I needed to cut my beard and hair as we were all getting lice. I knew that I could hire them out and make a profit. If only I knew how to do the deal.

I asked amongst the prisoners if any could speak Italian. I only needed the words for scissors and knife. By now we could all count in Italian, but that was about all. I had no luck. By three o'clock in the afternoon I had thought of what to do. I would draw them. I now needed something to draw on and draw with. It suddenly came to me: the cook. It took me no longer than a few minutes to find him. He was asleep and so I touched him on the shoulder.

"What do you want?" he asked in a rather unfriendly tone.

"I have something you want badly. Come with me." And I led him to the kitchen area, which being out of bounds, I could not have got to without him. I first gave him a smoke and then asked him for one of his ration boxes.

"Impossible," he said.

"We have to draw rations in them tomorrow. Anyway what do you want it for?" He was obviously curious.

I didn't reply. I had noticed a white apron hanging on a nail on the wall. "How many fags would you want for that apron?" I asked.

"It belongs to my mate," he replied, meaning the other cook.

"All the more reason for selling it." I replied.

"It will cost you 20 fags, but if you are found with it I shall say you nicked it and God help you then."

Thieving was about the worst crime possible in the camp. It would mean being thrown into a circle of men and having the living daylights punched out of you. This had to be because some would steal the rations of others. An apron, I felt, was

51

different. It was 'Iti' issue and nothing personal, so I took a chance.

From the fire in the kitchen I took some burnt wood. Now I could write and draw. I felt sorry for the sergeant. He stood there looking more than a little confused.

"What the hell do you want those for?" He asked.

"To clean my teeth." I replied, "Haven't you ever heard of charcoal being good for the teeth?"

"Oh yes, I suppose it could be." He murmured. Then with a second thought said, "Of course you could be going round the twist."

I grinned at that and walked out, having concealed the apron around my body and under my shirt. I then made for the toilet block. I tore off the tapes and bib. The tapes went down the toilet. I felt they might prove difficult to conceal if there was a search as it would be difficult enough to cope with the rest of the apron. I then set about my task.

On one side of the apron I drew a pair of scissors and on the other a knife. I folded this up with the remainder of the apron, for I knew it would be no use thinking of making a deal that night, as darkness would soon be upon us. The package was placed carefully under my mattress. I settled down for the rest of the evening and lit a cigarette.

After the morning count by the guards I made my way to the wire and sat there hoping for the same guard to pass by. Luckily I had only been there about 15 minutes when along he came. I took from my shirt the piece of apron and held it up showing him the scissors. He nodded his head as if in approval.

I held up both hands with my fingers and thumbs extended, showing that I would give ten cigarettes. He shook his head in disapproval then, quickly looked around to see that all was clear. He then stuck up his fingers so many times that I lost

Infantry Record Office,
E X E T E R.
4th September, 1942.

To:- Mrs. P. Reynolds,
　　　"Midge",
　　　　Colchester Road,
　　　　Lawford, Essex.

Madam,

　　　　I have to inform you that
your son's name - No. 6012060 Corporal
E.F. REYNOLDS, The South Wales Borderers -
appears in a list of British soldiers
broadcast from foreign wireless stations
and picked up in this Country.
　　　　The broadcast includes the
following message:-

　　　　　　"Quite well.　Thinking of
　　　　　you.　Fondest love to all -
　　　　　　　　Ben."

　　　　　I am,
　　　　　　　Madam,
　　　　　Your obedient Servant,

　　　　　　GM Seeks.

　　　　　　　　　　Lieut-Colonel
　　　　for Lieut-Colonel,
　　Officer i/c Infantry Record Office.

BP/RW.

A positive message from Ben in an otherwise negative situation.

53

count. He must have thought I was manufacturing them.

I just couldn't believe it.

I once more held up mine to denote that I would give 20 and at the same time I got up as if to walk off. He pointed to the spot where he stood as if to say we would meet there to do the deal. At the same time he babbled something in Italian, which meant nothing to me. He then walked away. Apart from when I went to get my Skilly I stayed at the wire all day. It seemed the only thing to do. He passed twice more in the morning and once in the afternoon but didn't even look my way.

Morning came once more with the count and my sitting by the wire. Within the hour, I saw him approaching from a distance. He was kicking at the sand as he meandered along. I felt quite excited as I felt a deal would be made. When he reached me he stopped, looked around, then from his pocket he withdrew a very respectable pair of scissors, about eight inches long. I took from my shirt two packets of cigarettes neatly tied with a thin strip of apron. We now had to make the exchange. Between us we had the curled barbed wire at least ten feet high and eight feet thick. I indicated to him to throw the scissors over, but he was not having that in case I fiddled him. We had stalemate.

I realised I had to make the first move. I placed a small stone under the tie and heaved the package over the wire hoping it would not fall amongst it. Fortunately it landed almost at his feet. He picked it up, checked that the cigarettes were within, and then tossed the scissors to me. Before I had the chance to show him the piece of apron with the knife drawn on it he had moved off.

I took the scissors into the building and got the fellow with the longest beard to cut off my hair as close as possible and my beard. I then did the same for him. He was delighted and so was I for we were both full of lice.

I charged him nothing for the treatment but just told him I would cut anyone's hair for one cigarette, firm of course, and beards for the same.

Naturally, word soon got around. I had my 20 cigarettes back by the next day. It was difficult to store these cigarettes, which came in individually so I would then cut a chap's hair for one firm, good quality and empty packet. This meant that one in eleven got a free haircut.

I was made.

I was busy making prison money: cigarettes.

I could not afford to employ an assistant but we had amongst us a dear old chap, or he appeared that way to me, although I think he wasn't over 45 years. He had been in the Merchant Navy. How he had got amongst us I never did think to ask him.

I was now in the position to buy my own bread and even cheese, and to smoke when I felt like it. I also had my friendly old sailor who would collect my Skilly and bread for me. At this time I was giving him three cigarettes a day. It was understood that he would keep his distance. I wanted no one to be too closely involved in my dealings. I needed a clear mind to think.

Chapter 7

DICING WITH LICE

My leg was playing up and was giving me some concern. The cut I had received during the rush for water hadn't, as I had first thought, healed completely. What started as no more than a small wet pimple had now grown to the size of a half crown coin. I felt really worried when I woke one morning after a night of little sleep because of the throbbing pain in the area of the wound.

I felt quite sick.

On closer inspection I found it was alive with tiny maggots.

I showed it to the RSM in charge of the camp and he said he would mention it to the Italian officer in charge of the count that morning. He did, but the reply was there was nothing he could do to help, as they had no suitable antibiotics.

I was inspecting the wound when my old sailor came up with my Skilly. He looked at the wound and said, "I can cure that for you, Corp. You will need sugar and soap to do the job. You will also need a bandage."

The bandage could be made from the rest of the apron. A small hard piece of Italian soap I had, and the sugar I could

56

buy from the Cook Sergeant—we only needed half a teaspoon. Sailor did the deal for the sugar with the Cook Sergeant for three cigarettes. I am sure he made one out of the deal but I couldn't blame him for that.

A burning glass was hired from its proud owner, who never let it out of his sight when on hire. This was a wonderful piece of equipment. I had tried to purchase it on many occasions, best thing in the world for lighting cigarettes.

The old sailor played the beam on the soap until it became pliable. He wound it round and round in his fingers, at the same time mixing in the sugar. When it was larger than the wound and about a quarter of an inch thick, he laid it on the piece of apron, which was to be the bandage. He then applied more heat with the glass until the soap and sugar were bubbling.

"This will burn the wound and the skin around it and it will hurt like hell," he said.

That was the understatement of the year.

"If you pull it off," he added, "It will be useless and you will be well into the gangrene stage. But if you can stick it for three or four minutes, the pain will ease."

I had no option. "Stick it on sailor and make it quick."

I honestly don't know how I stuck the pain. I felt dizzy and sick and I very much wanted to pass out. It felt as if he was gouging into the wound with a knife. After a while it didn't seem so bad. Nothing could be as painful as the initial two or three minutes.

"Right," said the old sailor. "We will repeat this each morning for at least three days."

The procedure was repeated the next day and from then on the wound began to mend. I gave him a loaf of bread for three days. He was delighted. The old 'sod' sold them for cigarettes. He told me that this was a treatment used in the days of the windjammers. He had heard of it from an old sailor who had served on one. I felt friendlier towards the old boy after this.

He was a small wiry individual, with a long pointed nose that always seemed to be running. I often wondered why he had not found a cure for that.

It was now some time towards the end of September 1942. The lice had well and truly arrived. Commonly known as crabs, they were digging themselves into the flesh wherever the body had any amount of hair at all. They laid their eggs in the seams of our clothes and multiplied their number daily by hundreds. We were nothing more than apes, sitting picking them out from each other's heads. The Camp RSM complained vigorously to the Italian officer and Camp Commandant. It was of little use. The guards were just as full of them as we were. They too were always scratching.

Two weeks passed and the Italians decided to send in a fumigator. I had never seen one of these before. It certainly looked as if it had come out of the Ark. It consisted of a large drum with a fire hole underneath, mounted on four large iron wheels. We were to stand in front of it, strip off stark naked and load our clothes into the thing until it was full. A wood fire burned below. If one's clothes were on the outside of the load you stood a good chance of killing off the lice but if they were in the middle you didn't as the heat was not sufficient. All it did was to incubate the eggs and within a couple of days we were just as badly off. It was a complete waste of time using it.

The Italians sent a party of their men to remove it. Once more they were pushing, shoving and shouting with the effort, for it certainly weighed a bit. And, moving it over sand didn't help any more than their gestures for us to help them.

To combat the lice, three Italians were sent into the camp with a large pair of shears each and once a week they would shear the heads and beards of all. This, of course, made my scissors obsolete. Back to the drawing board, I had to think again.

I got my piece of apron out and once more drew the knife on it and then, went off to find my crooked guard. I found him in the usual way and held up the drawing as before. I must admit it did look a bit like a weapon and that was probably exactly what he thought, because he shook his head in disapproval. Yet, at the same time, he pointed to the ground as if requesting a re-meet. No price was discussed. He just walked away.

The next morning the guard was there again. I couldn't believe my blinkers. There he stood holding up a cut throat razor. I felt that this must be of some considerable use and the deal was done for 20 cigarettes.

Now, I had to find a use for it. Within two days I had an idea. Would it be possible, if I made some dice, to encourage some to gamble with their cigarettes? There was only one way to find out. I broke a small piece of branch from a scraggy old bush tree, no more than the thickness of my thumb. I thought if I squared this up, it would finish about half an inch square, which would be big enough for what I wanted.

"Be careful how you use the razor, Corp," said the old sailor.

He explained that this type of metal was extremely brittle and would snap if not used carefully. I thought to myself, 'The old fellow knows a bit.' I had found him most useful in many ways and I felt I should change my attitude towards him. I had treated him more like a peasant or a servant, although this attitude was not my normal self.

I cut out the dice, and squared them up with the help of the nearest wall as a sanding block. It took time, but that really didn't matter; we seemed to have plenty of it. The portion of apron, which by now was quite unidentifiable, was washed well by sailor, and marked off into six equal squares. In these squares were marked the letters A.B.C.D.E.F. I cut the letters into the dice, but they were certainly not clear enough. Sailor said he would make some dye. This surprised me a bit. From my shirt and his own, he took the fattest lice and squashed the blood from them. After all, it was our blood. We began to fill in the letters on the dice with blood, which was really quite black.

Sailor went round the camp telling as many as possible that dice would be played at 2 p.m. We thought this to be the best time as most had a couple of hours sleep after Skilly.

By 1.30 p.m. a considerable crowd had gathered, most of them out of curiosity and the need for something different to watch. Bets were placed and I paid the odds, with cigarettes, according to the letters that showed uppermost on the dice. What with playing it on a sandy base, and all the tobacco falling out of the cigarettes with all the handling, it certainly wasn't a good plan. The RSM soon put a stop to it anyway. He told me to stop as it was against King's Regulations to gamble. I sold the dice, but not the cloth. I felt that might come in useful again one day.

Chapter 8

DEN OF INIQUITY

Time passed. We were now into October in 1942, and many were suffering from dysentery and malnutrition. Lots had already been removed from the camp half dead. Dysentery can really take it out of you, under the conditions in which we were held.

Dysentery is usually caused by eating contaminated food or from hands or objects. If it's left untreated, as in these cases, soldiers may pass over one litre of watery, foul-smelling diarrhoea per hour. This is accompanied by nausea, abdominal pain, rapid weight-loss and eventually the breakdown of their organs.

During our stay the Camp Commandant only paid us about five visits and each time he stopped our rations for the day, for something usually very petty. The reason was obvious. He had either sold the rations or hadn't any.

On his last visit it was quite amusing. I had been given a tip off that it was going to happen, so I was able to position myself to advantage.

He entered the camp in his usual well-pressed blue uniform and just as he was passing under one of the high windows he was covered with coffee dregs. These had been collected over a period of many days. The shock jolted him so much as to make one of his two cigarettes fall from his holder. He drew his small dress Beretta pistol from its holster and fired into the air with rage. I am confident he would have shot the culprit if he could have found him. We certainly didn't get any rations that day. This was OK for people such as me, but some of the fellows really needed them badly. Our RSM was never amused about incidents such as this.

It was rumoured on the same day that we were to be moved. This caused considerable excitement, but within 48 hours the rumour died, as did one dog belonging to the Italian officer. The dog became over-friendly and came in for a visit, never to depart. In return for one share, the cook agreed to cook it. My eighth share tasted absolutely fantastic. I had not tasted anything like it for a long time. On reflection, one cannot feel pleased about the event and I have no wish to enlarge upon it. It was nothing more than survival.

The official order came that we would be moving out the next day. Just think, only one day's notice. We were all issued with a second-hand blue-green Italian shirt already full of lice. We were told we would be moving out before Skilly. This would save the Commandant another ration supply. Loaded into trucks, we were taken to the railhead to be delivered by train to the port of Tripoli.

The delay in loading us onto the train was terrible. We did not get away until the late afternoon. Then the journey seemed to take some two hours or more. We assumed we had arrived when the train stopped and we could once more hear a lot of shouting. But, unfortunately for us, we were to stay in the cattle trucks for the remainder of the night. The door was opened just before dusk and an old five-gallon type drum was pushed in. This was to be used as a toilet.

The night was diabolical. No light, little ventilation, apart from the small openings from iron bars at the top of the verticals of the wagons. There was nothing to eat and the stench was beyond belief. By morning the bucket was overflowing. I felt that nothing could be worse than this, but I was wrong.

Daylight had broken when we were unloaded from this den of iniquity and were formed up on the quayside. It was difficult to believe our eyes. We had never seen so many prisoners. There were South African, Indian, Free French and us. There must have been a lot of POW camps in that area and they had brought all prisoners here, to load them aboard ship for transportation to Italy. I remarked to the old sailor on what a sorrowful sight they looked.

"Well Corp you haven't looked in the mirror lately. We are all the same." I realised this to be true.

We were ushered to the gangplank for boarding the ship.

On boarding her she appeared to be no more than a cargo ship with two holds: one for'ard, and one aft. She was certainly a small ship. The holds were opened at one point only and men were climbing down a vertical ladder onto the deck below.

Something seemed to tell me to hold back. I needed time to think. I had seen holds such as this on our own ships and that once down there, one could travel fore or aft. Both positions would be well away from the hatch cover, which would not be at all good with no sanitation etc. As each man reached the hold entrance he was given a tin of meat and a four-inch biscuit as before.

I said to sailor, "We will keep moving back and when you think the hold is nearly filled up we will arrive at the hatch cover. We can then position ourselves at the bottom of it."

"That's alright," he replied, "But if they don't batten down and we hit dirty weather we shall get soaked with spray and freeze to death."

He nearly convinced me that he was right, but I thought better of it. "You please yourself," I said, "But I am entering about last." I was pleased I did, as it turned out. I kept an eye open for sailor but I didn't see him again and I really missed him.

I was amongst the last 20 or 30 to enter the hold. It was not too difficult to hang about at the foot of the ladder. How many there were in that hold I never did find out, it was really packed tight. One could sit down but that was about all. A lot of hysterical talking and laughter was going on caused by fear and nervous tension, not knowing what would happen to us. The heavy hatch covers were placed over the hold with just a small opening left at the top of the ladder. At least I could see the sky and I felt a little safer, for had anything gone wrong, I could at least climb up the ladder first and have some sort of a chance.

The trouble with being a prisoner of the Italians was that they just didn't care about us. We were a nuisance and were neglected all the time.

It was dark before the ship moved off. It was pretty miserable and the throb of the engines made it worse, as if they were closing in on one the whole time. Heaven only knows how long we were on this boat. It seemed like a lifetime, but could not have been more than three days.

On this ship we were treated like animals so we had no alternative but to act the same. If we wanted to relieve ourselves we had no option but to carry out the movement where we sat and considering many had dysentery you can imagine what it was like. The stench at first was unbearable but I suppose one gets used to anything in time.

There was nothing we could do about it, so we just learnt to live with it. An Italian guard looked down from above. I shouted to him to protest about our conditions but I might just as well have dropped dead as he just swung his arm indicating to me to shut up.

The Mediterranean wasn't so kind either. We had a squall and that upset many and made them violently sick. There was little chance of freezing to death as sailor had suggested. The body temperature of the men made the hold quite unbearable.

The next day, and quite frequently from then on, water was passed down to us in containers by rope. Thank goodness they sent it down frequently; otherwise many would have gone without, for it was difficult to pass it round without spilling it. Those who were seasick just went without. They appeared dead for all practical purposes.

At one stage there was a considerable commotion and shouting from the blackness well into the hold. In minutes, I found out what it was all about. Some of them were passing a dead body along to the only bit of light where I sat, at the foot of the ladder. Those of us sitting at the bottom of the ladder had this body to cope with. And, we certainly didn't want it on our laps, but we had no option. I finished up with the feet.

I suggested to those around me that we should shout in unison to attract the attention of the guard above. This we did and a face appeared at the opening. The first thing that went through my mind was that it must stink up there what with the stench belting up from the hold. Yet the guard made no attempt to cover his mouth or nose. We shouted to him that we had a dead man below. He seemed not to understand what we were shouting about. I realised there was only one thing to do: climb the ladder and by sign language and movement demonstrate that the man was dead. The climb would be about 18 to 20 feet.

When I was half way up the ladder the guard shouted. I looked up and he was pointing his rifle straight at me. I stopped. Then I made another mistake. I let go with both hands to indicate the limpness of our dead man. The next thing I knew I was on top of those sitting at the foot of the ladder.

At least they broke my fall.

Although nothing in the way of injury came my way, unfortunately I did break the shoulder of one of those I landed on. Normally one could laugh over an incident such as this but then it was quite the opposite. The men I had landed on swore at me vehemently and the whole thing made me more livid than I already was.

Straight up the ladder I went again. I could not have cared less this time. I hated that bastard at the top. If he shot me, OK. I would be out of that bog below. Before one could say "knife" I was on the deck.

It is quite impossible to explain the feeling. The sky was a beautiful bright blue, flecked with puffs of white clouds. The sea was literally alive. The fresh air penetrated down into my lungs and made me feel as if I would suffocate if I took one more deep breath.

I have never experienced anything like it before or since.

For how long I stood taking in all this beauty I don't know, but I was brought back to reality by the guard poking me with his rifle and at the same time screaming blue murder. Three others joined him and I was being pushed back into the hold. I could imagine going down there headfirst. I would have sooner gone over the side into the lovely clear sea. They stopped pushing when a fair-haired civilian came up. He was about 55 years of age and he was for sure a member of the crew—the equivalent to our Merchant Navy.

"Do that again Englishman and they could well push you over the side," he said, speaking to me in English.

"Who the hell was this?" I thought. I had never seen a fair-haired Italian before. I always expected to find them with dark complexions. "Tell them I mean no trouble," I said, "We have a dead man below and would like him pulled up."

He translated what I had said. The guards just shrugged their shoulders, as if to say what could they do about it. The fair-haired one raised his voice and crossed himself, as if to say God help you when the time comes. This seemed to do the trick. One of them went off and came back five minutes later with an Italian officer who turned out to be quite reasonable. The situation was explained to him by the fair-haired one and the answer translated back to me. A rope would be brought and the corpse removed. One of the guards indicated to me to return to the hold. I told the fair-haired one to tell him that I would convey the orders to those below for the purpose of tying. He co-operated and did just that.

I felt the longer I could stay on deck the better for me, as every minute up there I felt was so important. Eventually the rope was lowered and the body pulled up most unceremoniously. It was spinning and bumping against the steel ladder. The rope was tied around his ankles.

I thought, "What an awful way to go."

Down below, in the hold, the body had been just a bundle to be disposed of anyhow and as quickly as possible, but seeing it, on deck, in the bright sunshine changed my attitude completely. It belonged to someone—a sweetheart, a wife, most certainly a mother. I felt very sad and wanted to cry.

I was soon jolted back to reality by one of the guards pointing in the hole in the hatch for me to go down. I hated that son of a bitch and all he stood for. There was no reason for that man to have died. He was entitled to reasonable treatment as a prisoner of war and they should have given it to him.

I returned to the hold after having been on deck for a good hour. I was able to tell those around me what it was like. It certainly helped to pass the time for them.

We must have been on the boat for four nights. It was early morning when the engines stopped. We had arrived at our unknown destination, which turned out to be Naples. After a couple of hours the hatches were removed completely and those who could manage it climbed the vertical ladder. Those who couldn't climb were winched up on a square platform.

We were lined up on the quayside and we must have looked a very poor sight, filthy dirty and stinking with human excreta where we had sat amongst it.

I noticed a large fire hose was being rolled out some distance from where I was now sitting. To my horror I realised that they were going to hose us down. My cigarette store was in the inside of my shirt. How was I to keep it dry? I had 20 packets with ten cigarettes in each. I had to think quickly, otherwise they would be ruined and this could jeopardise my survival. Terror struck me at the thought of losing them.

The cigarettes were already wrapped in my piece of apron. I immediately took off my spare Italian shirt, which I had been issued with before leaving Tarhuna (I had been wearing two to avoid having one nicked). I folded and wrapped the cigarettes as firmly as possible in this.

The hose was approaching.

I held the bundle behind me as firmly as I dared to avoid crushing it. The water from the hose hit the front of me from head to toe and at some considerable force. It was also salt water. I now had another problem, for after they had hosed the front, they expected us to turn around to hose the back. This wasn't on as far as I was concerned; the continuous flow of water would have soaked my bundle of fags.

So, I just stood there. They shouted, but I didn't move.

One of the guards walked with a threatening attitude towards me. The other lowered the hose. This was the pause I needed. I turned immediately with my back to the hose and my bundle held now against my stomach. I was feeling quite pleased. I had won that round.

Chapter 9

CAMPO PG70

We then shambled off to a nearby siding, as the odd brick was heaved at us by the local dockworkers, and once more, we were loaded into railway cattle trucks. We'd still had nothing more to eat apart from the tin of Bully type beef and biscuit that was issued on boarding the boat. The Italians were hopeless administrators. As one chap commented at the time, "They couldn't organise a bunk up in a brothel!" I was starting to wonder how much more we could stick of this. It was rumoured that many died on the trip and were just pushed over the side. I was quite prepared to believe this.

By late afternoon we arrived at another station siding, were unloaded and reloaded into trucks once more and then taken to our first official Prison of War camp. This was situated just outside Rome. Here, there were plenty of guards—real old-timers, but nevertheless guards. They were wasting their time, for not one of us could have escaped. We were all too knackered.

The camp consisted of new wooden huts with nice wooden floors and rows of double-tier bunks down both sides of the room. Windows opened, as any window should. There were 12 bunks on each side, which meant 48 men to the room. At the end there was a small room for two. This was for the Hut Commanders, usually two Sergeant Majors or RSMs. On each bed was placed a cardboard box about 18 inches by 10 inches by 6-8 inches deep. Oh dear, what joy it was. A British Red Cross parcel, although we didn't know it at the time for we had not seen one before.

The British Red Cross and the Order of St John were invaluable to the health, social and morale welfare of soldiers, civilians and their families in the Second World War. By 1946 they had reportedly raised 54 million pounds, which enabled them to send messages, food parcels and medical support. Up to 20 million food parcels were packed by mainly British, Canadian and later USA volunteers. They were then transported to the International Red Cross headquarters in the neutral territory of Geneva, Switzerland before being moved on to their destinations of need. The parcel included:

- *¼ lb packet of tea*
- *Tin of cocoa powder*
- *Bar of milk or plain chocolate*
- *Tinned pudding*
- *Tin of meat roll*
- *Tin of processed cheese*
- *Tin of condensed milk*
- *Tin of dried eggs*
- *Tin of sardines or herrings*
- *Tin of preserve*
- *Tin of margarine*

- *Tin of sugar*
- *Tin of vegetables*
- *Tin of biscuits*
- *Bar of soap*
- *Tin of 50 cigarettes or tobacco (sent separately—usually Player's brand cigarettes, or Digger flake pipe tobacco).*

There seemed to be nothing one could want for after receiving a Red Cross parcel. They varied a little, but whether Canadian or British, the contents were always welcomed.

The bunks were wooden slatted, in lieu of springs, but the mattresses were so thick you could well imagine you were at home again. There were also hot and cold showers in the camp, for which we were paraded before turning in for the night. This was a luxury. We were given a thin small towel each and a small piece of soap. Many were too ill to enjoy it all and were taken away. My reaction was if this is prison, I could stick it nicely until the end of the war.

The Italian officer in charge of our sector warned us about over-eating from the parcels, but the advice went like water off a duck's back. Mixing condensed milk with jam and chocolate was no good for any human system that had received nothing like it for months. Everyone was sick including my good self. Even the next morning I still felt ill. That night I clearly remembered having a nightmare. Witches were holding me over a large stew pot and were ladling the soup into my mouth until I was bursting open.

We had not been in this camp for more than three days when we were told we would be moving the next day. It turned out that we should never have been in this camp. It had been set up to receive a batch of officer prisoners. Even the parcels were meant for them. The camp was alive with senior Italian officers. There had definitely been a clanger dropped somewhere along the line, but to our advantage this time. We certainly left them a memento of our visit: crabs. You could be assured that they would be in the mattresses even after one night, let alone three.

We were to be moved to another camp for other ranks, this time further north. We were moved by road, then rail, and then road again to Campo PG 70 at Monte Urano, below Macerata, near the Adriatic coast. We had travelled through the night. The old train kept stopping, sometimes for quite a long time. We eventually arrived at the camp about noon the next day, after what was quite a pleasant journey; we had the remains of our Red Cross parcels and at least we were clean, apart from the lice of course.

Campo PG 70 was a much larger complex. It consisted of 15 main buildings within the wire and it held some 2,500 prisoners. The buildings were constructed from concrete blocks with heavy asbestos-type roofs. They were single storey. From the floor to the ceiling was a considerable height, once more

A Red Cross parcel was often shared between 2 and even up to 4 men.

built for fruit storage. Each building was about 240 feet long and 50 feet wide and at the end of each unit was a Cookhouse, as in Tarhuna.

The buildings were allocated: nine to the ranks of sergeant and below, four to the rank of sergeant major and above and one was divided to give the few officers we had in the camp their own section. One large building was an Italian store, once more within the perimeter, and one building was empty as if in reserve. In the other ranks' buildings were ten rows of triple-tier bunks, eight in each row, a three-foot space between each triple bunk and a six-foot gangway running between the rows.

The camp was surrounded by coiled barbed wire—eight to ten feet high and eight feet thick. There was also a clear area of some 15 feet and another fence of barbed wire of the same height, but single stranded and held with wooden posts. Beyond this again was a high wall with barbed wire on the top. In one particular area there was only the wall with the barbed wire. At each corner of the camp there was a tall sentry box or lookout some 20 feet high, with a search light and machine gun, manned by day by one guard and at night by two.

Rations were drawn daily by voluntary fatigue parties and taken to individual cookhouses. The food was prepared and cooked by the appointed cooks for each building. It was usually Skilly, but was much thicker with vegetables and the portion of cheese was larger in our weekly ration. The bread and quantity were the same, but we did get the Red Cross parcels, if we were lucky, once a fortnight but usually it was every three to four weeks.

Life in the camp was boring and very cold at nights, although we had two blankets each. Once a fortnight we were given a form on which we could write a letter home. If you were unlucky enough it could take you a week or more to write

Dear Dad.

Its quite a while since I wrote to you but I guess you get news from home to say that I'm OK. I'm quite well in myself. I'm looking forward to the figs you sent me. I shall be glad when the day come dad that we may once more be all together again. How many times I have recalled your words to me I really do not know, a thousand times I should think, never no more will I complain or grumble like I use to remember how I use to be so perticular at the table now again. I've asked Ena to send me some socks.

Its a lovely day to-day nice and hot I suppose the weather is getting nice at home now, don't you?

I often wonder how brother Bill is getting on. We have a marvelous time really and decent food, write and tell mum that, also brother Len in the marines if you no were he, is poor old Len Ha! Ha! Cheerio dad Ill carry on OK. Your loving son. Ben.

Times were hard and being able to write home certainly helped.
Letter written by Ben to his father, CPO Arthur Reynolds, whilst he was serving on HMS Wildfire.

75

it, as it was difficult to borrow a pen or pencil; these were issued to the Camp RSM by the Italians but somehow only a few were provided.

Being able to write home certainly helped, especially for my parents, as I had been posted as missing and the receipt of my personal letter must have relieved them of any doubt. Later, I gathered, they had been told that my name had been broadcast over the radio and picked up by the Red Cross.

This now meant that one would get the occasional letter from home and believe it or not, I should think that it would not be exaggerating to say, that these were read at least a hundred times.

"I shall be glad when the day comes dad that we may once more be all together again. How many times have I recalled your words to me, I really do not know. A thousand times I should think. Never no more will I complain or grumble."
  —Extract from a letter written from Ben to his father

Chapter 10

GOD SAVE THE KING!

Tin bashing became a full-time occupation for most of us, and to do this one had to have tins. These were collected from the Red Cross parcels. It was also necessary to have a pair of scissors. I was very lucky as I still had mine. The tins were opened up and flattened out. The edges turned and joined together with other tins and the finished product was a metal attaché case, complete with hinges. When you think the only tool was a pair of scissors, the bench was the edge of your bed, and the hammer was one of the battens off the bed, it wasn't a bad result.

Time passed quickly on this job. We would draw our Skilly at 12 noon, and it was an unwritten law that no one started bashing again until two o'clock and finished at five o'clock in the evening. If they didn't cease, a mighty roar from all in the building would go up and the bashing would stop immediately. Cigarettes could be earned this way by selling the cases to the guards who must have sold them outside the camp.

State of the war in North Africa

Ben was captured on June 18th 1942, prior to Rommel seizing Tobruk. But Rommel's triumph was just a forerunner to defeat in the face of a new Allied adversary, General Bernard Law Montgomery.

On August 13th, 1942, Montgomery took control of the Eighth Army and his tenacious, 'no withdrawal' policy helped to transform the mindset of the Allies. Under Montgomery's leadership, the Allies, which included courageous Australian and New Zealand forces, went on to win the Second Battle of El Alamein. It was the end of October and in November US troops landed in Tunisia.

Christmas came and went and we would never have known it, apart from the weather being very cold. We kept within the building, apart from the usual early morning and evening roll call.

The English Major, in conjunction with a body of RSMs, decided that it might be a good idea if we had a concert, something that would be quite possible with so many different types around us. Discussion groups were formed to put forward ideas. I had nothing to do with this as I felt I could neither sing nor act, so had little to offer. Within two months the show was put on in the empty building. The only difference was at the first show one had to stand apart from the officers and Regimental Sergeant Majors. It certainly was very good and went on for at least ten days.

The scenery was terrific. It was made from pieces of cardboard and the old tea chests that the Red Cross parcels came in. The script was written by a couple of prisoners. The

Italians kindly produced a piano and some prisoners dressed up as women for the part and looked terrific. As to where they got the wigs and dress material from I can only imagine that someone had influence with the Italian Commandant. We had two different shows during our stay.

I got to know a corporal who worked on the scenery. He turned out to be a decent friend. We were not in the same block, but I saw him frequently. He was a 'Digger', and one of the Australian 'Desert Rats'.

For some reason, after the theatre activities came the queers. Whether it was due to the dressing up as women, I don't know, but from then on it wasn't unusual to see lovemaking by two men. The Italians would get livid over this. They caught a couple at it one day and put them into a prison cell in the outer perimeter. The joke was that they had put them in the same cell for a week.

General Bernard Law Montgomery in a Grant tank November 1942 watches his tanks move up.
Credit: E 18980 from the collections of the Imperial War Museums.

It was noticed by some that women came into the camp to work in the Italian offices and when they finished they just walked past the guard at the outer gate. This gave one of the prisoners the idea of doing the same. Apparently, he joined up with the fatigue party for collecting rations and once in the store in the outer perimeter, he took off his coat and put on one of the theatre company's wigs and dress, and made for the main gate. He had a small problem. He was flat footed to start with and he still had the army boots on which he was wearing when he was captured. He was also short and round. However, I gather he made it to the gate and actually walked through without the elderly sentry noticing anything amiss. Unfortunately, a few yards further on, he was confronted by an Italian officer and marched back, with his ear firmly clamped between the forefinger and thumb of the officer. He had a job to live that one down.

Various attempts to escape were made without success, and as this caused trouble for the camp, the word was passed around officially that no more individual attempts should be made, without the permission of a newly formed escape committee. This consisted of the English Major and a couple of RSMs. Nothing like this had at this time entered my mind. It didn't seem very practical to escape. It seemed a long way to Switzerland and I couldn't see where else one could have made for. As yet, the Allies had not made a landing in Italy.

I noticed that a large marquee had been brought in and erected on the waste area, between the buildings and the wire. It was said that it was to house prisoners who were suffering from dysentery and other diseases. I did not give it another thought. It turned out eventually that it was the brainchild of my friend Digger, with the co-operation of the Escape Committee they had persuaded the Italians that this was necessary to avoid spreading disease. But it was used for nothing more than an earth store. From inside this marquee they were digging a tunnel, using the tea chests from the Red Cross parcels for the shell.

The whole thing was dug, discovered and back filled before I heard anything about it. It was a well-kept secret. It was thought afterwards that the Italians knew what was going on and just let it continue until they were ready to strike. I mentioned it to Digger and that was when he told me the full story. He spent ten days in solitary for his part. I gather he was actually caught in the tunnel. One week later, a South African was found hanging by the neck from the cistern in one of the toilet blocks. It was said that he had divulged the secret of the tunnel to the Italians.

9th Australian Infantry Division in a posed photograph during the Second Battle of El Alamein 1942 (photographer: Len Chetwyn) advancing through the dust and smoke of the battle.
Credit: E 18474 from the collections of the Imperial War Museums.

We had about 500 South Africans in the camp; they were kept in two separate blocks. They were not liked by the British prisoners and always got better treatment and better food.

An announcement was made over the camp tannoy system that those of the Catholic faith who would like to attend service would parade at the main gate at 10 a.m. on Sunday morning. I was not a Catholic but something seemed to tell me to attend, so I did. We were marched out of the inner perimeter to the outer, to a building that had been converted into a temporary place of worship for the Italian staff, their wives and children. I knew nothing about what was going on but felt it made a change, and there were nice looking girls amongst the congregation. The most important thing of all was, at the end of it, we prisoners were handed a loaf of bread and a bunch of grapes. Our names were also taken so that the next week, when we paraded, the roll was called to prevent any 'non-believers' jumping on the bandwagon. During one of these sessions we were given a four-page pamphlet with some prayers printed inside and on the back was 'God Save The King' in big print. I never did know what that was all about but it helped me later on.

Victory to the Allies in North Africa

By the spring of 1943, the German and Italian forces had capitulated and North Africa was in the hands of the Allies. The Allies recognised this advantage and moved swiftly across the Mediterranean from North Africa to grasp the island of Sicily.

Victory to the Allies—a Churchill tank and other vehicles parade through Tunis, May 8, 1943.
Credit: NA 2880 from the collections of the Imperial War Museums.

Chapter 11

MAJOR DISGUISE

Somebody, somehow, somewhere in the camp had by hook or by crook built a radio, as we were getting regular morning bulletins passed by word of mouth. The Allies had invaded Sicily. This was around the first week of July.

The Allies landed in Sicily on the 10th July 1943. I had now been a POW for 13 months. I was determined that as soon as I heard they had landed in Italy, I would do everything within my power to get away from these blasted prisons. I was finding them more than difficult to tolerate.

My Digger acquaintance came up to me and offered me the chance to help cut through the sewer to freedom. Apparently the sewer was just about big enough to crawl along, if you were not too big. But the snag was, every-so-often, there were iron bars sticking down from the top to prevent this and exactly how many, they were not sure.

The idea was to cut them away with the use of a hacksaw, which they had acquired. They also didn't have the permission of the Escape Committee. Apparently they did not want it to leak out into the South African compound. I had no option but to decline this kind offer as, to coin a phrase, I'd had enough of other people's shit! I also had to get some gear together for my own escape, if it were to be. They did, however, suffer this task for a fortnight then gave it up. It was too demoralising and not only that, they couldn't continue because the supply of hacksaw blades dried up.

We had heard through the radio that Italy's dictator, Benito Mussolini had fallen from power and that Victor Emmanuel had asked Marshal Badoglio to form a Government on the 26th July. For me, this meant that the time for moving out was not far away.

A working party went daily to the outer perimeter to work in the workshop. Apparently they made packing cases. With little difficulty I persuaded one of their number to stay behind and to allow me to take his place for one day. This cost me a loaf of bread, which he would have received for working, plus my loaf of bread and whatever fruit I was given for attending church the following Sunday.

I had to have a look around. I did not know why, but something was telling me to do this. It turned out to be quite easy. I was counted through the gate with the others and marched to the workshop. The workshop was a large area filled with lengths of rough sawn boards cut to the required lengths. Three prisoners worked together, nailing and battening the boards together to make a large rectangular box. There were four or five guards wandering around. They seemed very concerned, and then they formed a group and started walking away. It was the current dire situation of their country that worried them.

During our break one old fellow came over. He said he had worked in America. He obviously wanted to be friendly and his English was reasonable, with a strong Italian and American accent. I thought I would test him and possibly took a chance of being clobbered in doing so.

"Antonio, come here." I said, beckoning with my finger.

He came over, all smiles. I was pleased about that. This was the reaction I was hoping for, as I didn't know his name and all Wops were called Antonio or Bastard as far as we were concerned. And they knew it.

"My name is Benito," he said.

"God help you when the English get here." I said, drawing my finger across my throat and then crossing myself, at which by now I was quite good.

"Why?" he replied. "I have always been very good to all POWs. Nobody can say anything against me."

"I can." I replied. "But on the other hand I can help you too."

His face lit up. This meant to me that he had been a bastard to someone at some time. "How can you help me? And may I call you by your first name?" he asked.

"Call me Corp," I replied.

I don't know to this day how I thought of the following but it just came out without even having to think. "You see these two stripes on my arm? Well you mustn't tell anyone else, but they mean nothing. I am a British Major and I am here for the sole purpose of seeing how our prisoners are being cared for. As you may know I have only been in the camp for two weeks and there are others here like myself."

He was stupid. He listened like a child and believed it.

"Now take me on a conducted tour of this workshop and if you do what I ask, I will give you a note signed by myself to say that you helped the British in the camp, and that you are not to be touched. Do you understand?"

"You had better pick up some wood and follow me," he said.

The two POWs with whom I had been working looked at me with complete bewilderment. I felt sure they believed it as well.

I picked up a couple of four-foot planks and off I went with Benito. What the hell I was looking for, I did not know. But, then I saw a pair of navy-blue trousers made from a denim material. I put my wood down and held them up. They were no way near big enough.

"Right," I said to Benito, "I want a pair like these but big enough to fit me."

"Tomorrow I will get you a pair," he said.

On a bench lay a jumble of tools. I took a brace and a bit, a pad saw and a pair of pinchers. At the time I really didn't know why.

By then I felt I had taken enough chances, so handing him the tools I turned to the guard and said, "Bring those into the camp tomorrow with the trousers and I will write your slip, if you bring the paper and pen." He made no protest at all. He just seemed to accept it all. I joined my two workers and when we had finished we were marched back to the camp. That night I lay on my bed wondering whether or not I had done the right thing. What if he had second thoughts about it all and reported it to the Camp Commandant? They could have shot me as a suspected spy, anything for an excuse. Three or four times I woke in the night and wondered about it.

The following morning threw a different light on the whole thing. I got to the gate and saw the chap I had taken over from the day before and said to him, "You have a guard out there called Benito. Tell him to meet the Major outside the theatre block at 11 a.m. If he can't make it at that time, then on the hour from then onwards."

"OK, Sir," he said, which left me a bit puzzled to say

the least. Benito turned up at 11 a.m. sharp, much to my surprise, complete with tools but no trousers.

"I will bring the trousers tomorrow at the same time," he said.

"That will be fine," I replied. "And I will give you your note then."

He looked a bit taken back. I felt sure he thought I was going to trust him. The trousers came the next day and quite a good pair they were too. I took the pen and paper from him and wrote:

> *"To our gallant Allies. The holder of this note has been a very good Italian and has helped the British troops whenever he has had the chance. By the authority bestowed upon me by the King of England, I order that this man shall <u>not</u> be hanged by the neck until dead."*

I signed it 'British Representative, Mediterranean Forces.'

He read the note, took my hand and kissed the back of my fingers. He was almost in tears. I thought I had better take advantage of this and told him to bring me a shirt within two days, at the same time and place, and the shirt must be a similar colour. Believe it or not, he did. I was now made for escape, at least as far as clothes were concerned.

Chapter 12

OUT OF THE FRYING PAN...

As I said before, normally we would be awakened by the shout, 'Out, out, roll call!' But this particular morning there was not a murmur. There wasn't a single Italian to be found anywhere in the camp. This was fantastic. My first thought was that the war was over, and we were on our way home any day, but how wrong I was.

The officers, assisted by the RSMs, took over the camp. One of them could type and for the remainder of the day orders were continually being pinned up on a notice board. One said:

'The Italians have capitulated and the camp is now under the Command of the British Major' (who had appointed himself as Camp Commandant).

I found this to be somewhat bewildering, as did many others. Another notice pinned up stated:

'Under no condition is anyone allowed to the leave the camp. The Allies will arrive within a matter of days to take everyone away. There was nothing to escape from, so anyone leaving the camp will be court-martialled on return to the UK, as a deserter'.

This lot took some swallowing. It was like jumping from the frying pan into the fire. I never saw this Major and I wondered sometimes if anybody else did. But he seemed to have the support of the RSMs.

Ben knew that there was a radio held secretly in the camp, but he was not to know that it had received secret orders.

Revealed in Tom Carver's book Where the Hell Have you Been? a regular, friendly, apparently benign BBC religious broadcast gave the following instructions transmitted in code:

"In the event of an Allied invasion of Italy, officers commanding prison camps will ensure that prisoners of war remain within camp. Authority is granted to all officers commanding to take necessary disciplinary action to prevent individual prisoners of war attempting to rejoin their own units."

When MI9 in London anticipated the surrender of the Italians to the Allies, what pray was to happen to the 80,000 Allied prisoners held in the Italian POW camps? These prisoners were malnourished and to release them without coordinated efforts was a concern. So it would seem that MI9 made the decision, without informing Winston Churchill, that they would issue an order referred to as the 'Stay Put'. By giving the order, it was anticipated that Allies landing in Italy would arrive at the POW camps,

take control and administer whatever care was required to
transport the Allied prisoners home. We must assume that
MI9 did not anticipate that the German troops travelling
down from the North of Italy might arrive at the POW
camps before the Allies, which is exactly what happened in
Campo PG70.

Of the 80,000 Allied prisoners in Italy 50,000 were
resecured by the Germans and moved to POW camps
in Germany and Poland where, suffering much harsher
conditions, many never made it home.

Within two days of this episode we awoke to find a load
of Germans in the camp and manning the sentry boxes. The
Germans meant business and they intended to continue as
they had begun. Up went more notices. Anyone attempting
to escape would immediately be shot. Curfew would be as
evening came and the siren would be sounded to tell us when.
Anyone outside of their buildings after that would be shot.
This meant back to the bucket. That night one could hear the
occasional chatter of machine gun fire from the sentry boxes.
This was to let us know that they were still there, just in case
anyone had fancy ideas of making a break.

After this, we never saw another Red Cross parcel, or letter
from home. The Jerry blamed the Americans and announced
over the tannoy that the reason was, "Because the Yankee
friends were sinking the Red Cross boats that were bringing
them." I realised that these fellows were not the Afrika Korps
troops, but must be a bunch of lunatics.

We heard once more from our own radio that the Allies had
landed at Salerno. If this were true, I felt it could not be long
before they would release us. It was now September and no
more news of any great interest was released. This upset the

morale considerably.

Digger came to me one afternoon and asked me if I would like to join him and some others in an arranged escape. Apparently, amongst the Germans were some Poles who had joined the German Army and one was very sympathetic towards the British. He had agreed to leave a small gate open in the wall. This was situated at the back of the theatre block. The escape was planned for 10 p.m. Now, escapes or anything

Map of Allied Invasion of Italy September 3, 1943.

else, are all right if one has actually planned them oneself, or had a meeting and discussed the details thoroughly. But one out of the blue like this was indeed quite disturbing.

The trip that night meant that I had got to stay in block 'F', which was Digger's block, instead of my own, block 'C'. Of course it didn't enter my head at the time on how I was going to get back to block 'C' the next morning if it wasn't successful. I spent the time from curfew until ten o'clock getting myself dressed in my trousers and shirt. I realised I was going to be somewhat cold, so I cut the sleeves and collar from my two old shirts, and donned them under my new one, which Benito had brought me. I then looked down at my British Army service boots and there was a sight to behold—my size 11s sticking out from the bottom of my rather short trousers. I felt something had to be done about

Sentry box: "Anyone attempting to escape would immediately be shot."

93

these. I took my razor knife, which was now becoming somewhat blunt, and cut off the tops. I left the tongue long, turned it down, and made a small hole in it and then laced it down. Smashing! They looked like a pair of brogues with rather large toecaps, but that could not be helped. I had an old sand bag for my gear. I was now ready to move.

Time seemed to drag, although there was only another hour to wait. I looked at my watch and wondered what I would be doing this time tomorrow night.

We moved off a few minutes before ten and, hugging the wall, made our way along the side of the block, across to the theatre block and then along the side of that. I really hadn't a clue. I just followed Digger. Blimey, I couldn't believe my

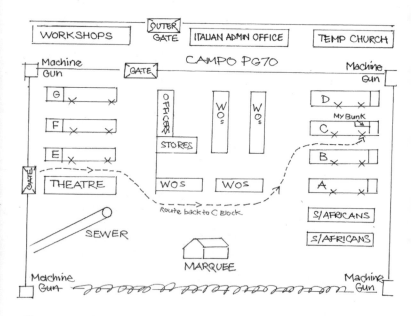

Illustration taken from Ben's sketch, Campo PG 70: "I ran like hell on the same route back."

eyes. There must have been 20 there.

"If this lot get out, I'll eat my hat." I grinned. I hadn't got one.

Ten minutes past. Nothing happened. There seemed to be one chap who was responsible for this effort. You could just see him go forward now and again and gently try the gate. I nudged Digger and flicked my thumb, suggesting we should go back. He shook his head in disapproval.

Then it happened. The searchlights came on from both ends and machine gun fire rattled against the wall of the theatre. I ran like hell on the same route back. Once around the end of the theatre I was comparatively safe from the firing. Don't ask me why, but I didn't stop running until I arrived at my own block 'C', which was on the other side of the camp. Throughout this run the whole camp was lit up and the bloody siren was going. I got to the big sliding doors of my block, which were kept closed at night and opened the small door, which was built into them. I literally fell through it and went straight into the three buckets that were kept there. Piss and shit flew everywhere, and so did I.

I will never forget the rumpus it caused. It woke up the whole of the building. Someone switched on the lights. That helped. I was straight down my alley, up onto my bunk and under the blankets before you could say knife.

One of the sergeants came along and asked me what I thought I was doing. I just said, "Put out the lights quick, the Germans are coming."

He reacted immediately and that was that, apart from the fellows around me saying I stunk.

The Germans came in the next morning to get us out for counting and saw the mess on the floor. They ordered those at that end to clean it up and I didn't hear the last of that.

I made it my business to contact Digger as soon as I could,

after the count, to find out what had gone wrong with the plan. He didn't know the answer to that, but he told me that only three of them got away, two were dead, four wounded and the remainder had been taken away. They did the right thing. They put their hands up and lucky for them the Jerry stopped firing. I spent the rest of the day watching my clothes and blankets dry. These I had washed. As I sat there, I thought to myself, any more escapes would only be of my own making.

Chapter 13

ESCAPE!

It was now the end of September. Naples had fallen to the Allies and Jerry had decided to move us.

Rumour had it that we were off to Austria. How was I to get out of this?

Hiding in the camp, I thought, but where?

It was said that within 24 hours we were to be loaded onto trucks and taken to a rail siding to be, once more, loaded into cattle trucks, for our move to Austria. I thought to myself, not this time. I had just about had as much as I could take of their flipping prisons. This time, somehow, I was going to leave them all behind and that made me feel really good. I was going home to see my girlfriend, Ena, and my family.

I was brought out of my daydreaming by Digger tapping my foot. "You know we are off tomorrow?" he said.

"So I gather," I said.

"But if you stay by me you won't be going far."

"How do you make that out?" he quizzed.

"Easy, I have the gear."

He looked at me as if I was off my head.

"I'm telling you now, stay with me and I guarantee that the only thing that will stop us making the escape will be a steel cattle truck and I doubt whether there are any of those around now."

"OK, I'm with you," and he nodded in agreement.

He was, as I have said, one of the 'desert rats'. He was also

Pocket sized photo of girlfriend, Ena, carried by Ben throughout the war.

a clever chap and could be well trusted. It was important to have someone like him at a time like this, for one could well be in a truck with 40 or 50 others and not one would show keenness to make a break.

Morning came and the Germans made their morning count. They then started moving us off by the block. Our block moved off at about 12 noon. This was much too early for me. I was afraid the train might move off early and I would travel too far before darkness fell. So, as we went past Digger's block, I just slid out of my group in to his crowd who were just milling round.

"Oh dear," he said.

"I thought you were going without me."

Now for a little bit of planning… the station could not be further away than it was when we arrived in the camp and that had taken about half an hour by road. So, if we stayed put and left with Block 'F' it might well work out better. On the other hand, there was little else we could do to change it.

We arrived at the station siding at about 4 p.m. The train was there with rather a lot of trucks. Many were already loaded. The guards were loading the prisoners, 50 to a wagon. Blimey! You couldn't move. There were also two buckets for 'the usual' and a container of oak apple coffee. That's what we thought it was anyway.

Paying special attention to what the guards were doing, I made a mental note that the lever on the side of the truck, which was swung over, was five boards up. The lever passed through an eye, and to stop it lifting again it was wired through a hole in the pin on the end. This was going to be a piece of cake. I had the gear.

We were herded into the truck which had the usual rectangular openings on the topside, covered with iron bars. By hoisting

Digger up now and again he could see what was going on.

It appeared that a guard would be travelling on a platform between the trucks, at intervals. Naturally, we had not checked for this, as we were not aware of it happening. Luckily, as it turned out, we did not have one on either side of our truck.

The object of these guards was, if any of them saw any movement by the track they would fire. It would snowball along the train. This would mean if you were seen to jump, your chance of survival would be small, for they all carried light machine guns.

It was dark when we moved off. I immediately started work. Five boards up and slightly to the right of the door opening, I drilled four holes with my brace and bit. I then took my pad saw and cut out a hole about four inches square, picked up my pinchers, stuck my hand through the hole, undid the wire and swung over the lever. All that was left to do now was to slide open the door. I eased the door gently open and at the same time looked out. The train started to slow down, as we appeared to be approaching a built up area. I realised the worst, a station was about to appear. I closed the door, put my hand through the hole and swung back the bar. But then, neither Digger nor I could find the piece of wire to hold it closed, despite the wire being quite thick. Now what?

"Give me some dregs from the bottom of that coffee as fast as you can." I called out.

Digger slowly tipped the coffee out and took from the bottom a handful of black coffee dregs. I thought the rest of them were going to lynch him, but luckily it was only those in the immediate area who had any idea of what he was up to, because they got wet arses.

Where I had cut the hole, the clean edges stood out too much to be healthy, especially if we stopped at this station. I couldn't take a chance. I carefully smeared the dregs onto the bare wood and it certainly helped the situation. The train stopped. Digger could see the guards walking out from between the trucks and then to my horror he said that some of them were checking the doors. I lowered him immediately and pressed my back against the precious hole I had cut in the side of the truck. The light was very faint, but I felt the hole would still show less, if covered from the inside.

It seemed like forever, squatting there with my back pressed firmly to the side of the truck. I suddenly had a thought, which made me feel very sick. If the hole was noticed and somebody stuck a bayonet into it, I would be right down the creek let alone up it.

We were lucky. After what seemed an eternity, the train moved off. I once more went through the procedure and opened the door slightly. I turned to Digger and said, "Behind my back I have the pinchers in one hand and the pad saw in the other. If you guess which hand correctly you will have the choice of going first or second."

He guessed wrongly so I elected to jump first. I looked out and thought the train was going a little too fast. Also, the area still seemed to be built up. Ten minutes passed. The train seemed to slow down again and the area certainly looked more rural.

Now! I thought. The advice I was once told by a prisoner who had undergone parachute training quickly went through my head: keep your feet together, knees slightly bent, elbows tucked in, fists clenched and held firmly across your chest, and feel free when you jump. Well, I still don't believe him. The last thing I remembered was Digger saying, "Are you going?"

I hit the embankment, rolled over and over, saw many

Chapter 14

ON THE RUN

The first feeling I had when I did come round was a feeling of extreme cold and wetness. I was lying amongst a bed of stinging nettles and long grass, and the ground was very wet. I eased myself up but found this movement rather difficult. I felt so sore and stiff. My hand was paining me terribly. If a German had walked passed I would have given myself up willingly. I laid there for what seemed an age, but it couldn't have been for it was still not properly light when I forced myself to get up onto my knees.

There, only a few yards away, was a small shed with wire all around it. Beyond this was a reasonably sized house and a couple of out-buildings. I felt I needed cover and made for the small shed. It was a chicken house. As I opened the door a few chickens rushed around and made their way out into the run. The noise frightened the life out of me. I lay down on the floor and went to sleep.

The next thing I remembered was being touched. It was a man, with a woman looking over his shoulder. I felt sick and very dizzy and could not react to the touch. My mind was blank. On reflection, it was a strange feeling, like coming out of anaesthetic. It was only when I heard the man say, "Where have you come from?" did I come to my senses.

I realised that it was of little use telling him anything but the truth. I told him I was a British Prisoner of War and had jumped from the train the night before.

"I will help you to my barn." He said.

The farmer, as I will call him, took my arm and helped me across the compound into the barn. He addressed the woman, whom I took to be his wife, in Italian. She went off and returned with a bowl of hot water and a towel. Under her arm she also carried a large frameless mirror. This she held up for me to look into.

It was the first time I had looked into a proper mirror since I had been taken prisoner. I could not recognise myself. My hair was chopped short. My face was much thinner than I would have thought. It was grazed, cut and black with cinder dirt mixed with the blood. The little finger on my right had been either broken or badly dislocated and the back of my hand was badly grazed.

The woman passed me the bowl to wash myself but eventually did it for me, as I just couldn't make the effort. I was given a bowl of hot, clear soup and a piece of bread. She also laid two handsome apples on the box beside me. I was confidant by now that all would be OK. I felt they would not call in the police or Germans.

The farmer asked me to get off the box on which I was sitting. He lifted the lid. It was like a large blanket box and it was empty.

"This is where I would like you to sleep. In the daytime if you hear any movement outside you must get straight in the box and close the lid. If it is one of us we will open the lid to let you know. But, if the Germans carry out a proper search, we shall tell them that we heard movement in the barn. We shall have to give you away because the penalty for harbouring POWs is death. They have made this quite clear on the radio."

I thanked him and said I understood and that I hoped to be away the next day.

I had been in the barn for two days when the farmer told me that a friend of his would be taking me into the hills to a safer place. Here we were somewhere between Pesaro and Senigallia. During the afternoon he called me out. There stood a horse and cart. I was to travel in the front with the man handling the reins. The farmer told me that if we were stopped I was to act dumb and to leave everything to the driver. I felt rather suspicious about this move. I felt they might be handing me over to the local police.

I was wrong.

We drove the old horse along the rather small roads and didn't see a single German. We eventually arrived at a farm, some five or six miles inland, as far as I could estimate. There was a shed at the lower part of the field adjoining the farmhouse and I was told to stay in the shed and only venture out at night. Food was brought to me three times daily. The coffee once more seemed as if it was made from acorns. It was always so bitter.

I stayed on this farm for some ten days and by then I was becoming very bored. Time seemed to drag on immeasurably. I only saw the man three times daily when he brought my food and we didn't share in any conversation because he never spoke. It was a matter of opening the door, putting the pot on a small box, which was used as a table and walking out again. He ignored me each time I spoke. It was very difficult to understand it all.

I was feeling fit again and when he brought the food in I just said, "I'm off first light tomorrow. Please try and get me a jacket." I hadn't a clue whether he understood me or not. He obviously did because he returned in less than an hour with a heavy pullover with roll neck and sleeves. He passed it to me and smiled. I was quite confused and felt as if I wanted to question him, but thought better of it.

Dawn came and the sun was rising by the time I moved off. I had my watch and this proved very useful—I really only had the sun to guide me south and it was rather important to know the time of day, combined with the position of the sun. I was extremely cautious when I first moved off because, apart from moving south, I hadn't a clue what I was up to. I certainly had not experienced anything like this before. I made sure to keep off the roads and walked on the tracks and open land. At least I felt if I did come up against any Huns I might be taken for a farm worker. I had it in my mind that if this did occur I would produce a limp as if I were crippled and act stupid and dumb: the dumb bit I had got from the farmer, the stupid bit I got from the mirror because nobody anywhere near sane looked like me.

Time passed and the air grew damp. I walked until dusk and settled down in a copse to sleep, having no real idea how far I had covered. I estimated something like nine miles plus, because I was only dawdling. I was grateful for the pullover, as the nights were cold. I realised then that there certainly were some good Italians around.

The sun woke me after a cold night attempting to sleep. It was always the way. I dropped off to sleep when it was time to get up. I continued like this for three days and by this time I was starving. But I had been hungry before and as there was always water to be had, it didn't worry me. It is not until you have been without water that you suffer more. You can do without food for much longer.

On the fourth day I saw a village in the distance. I had a reasonable smattering of Italian and a few lire in my pocket; I would take a chance and try to buy some bread. I walked along the first road I came to and within five minutes was amongst civilisation. The first place of business I came to was a vino bar, which was situated amongst a row of rather dilapidated private cottages. I looked through the window and seated on plain wooden benches were three old men very poorly dressed; the fella behind the bar did not look much different. So, I entered and walked up to the bar, "Una litre vino, prego," I said.

I am sure I would have done as well if I had made my request in sign language. The barman looked at me in bewilderment and the three old fellows stopped talking and looked towards the bar. I repeated the order and started to wish I had never entered. I was not afraid but I felt such an idiot. He drew off the vino from a large barrel into a badly chipped heavy glass jug. I placed the lire I had on the counter and then he pushed them back to me. This was interesting. He was not that stupid. He had a good idea of what I was up to. I asked for some bread. He shook his head and pointed to the door, at the same time babbling something I could not understand. I guessed he did not want me on his premises.

But the vino tasted fantastic and as always warmed my head and my heart. I had almost finished the vino when the door opened behind me and in came an old Italian policeman (Carabinieri), with a rifle slung over his shoulder by the shoulder strap. It was made of black leather. I wondered then, as I had often before, why the Italians used leather when the

107

British Army used webbing. I much preferred the leather.

He walked within three feet of me before he spoke. That was his first mistake. I hadn't any idea what he was talking about as he was speaking too quickly. He seemed excited and from his manner appeared quite confident about something. The barman was looking rather sick in the face as the policeman was addressing the conversation to him and me. The three old chaps got up and left. Oh dear, these were definitely warning signals and I felt then that the policeman was certainly being hostile.

He directed his gaze straight at me at the same time raising his voice. Then he made his second mistake—he started to remove the rifle from his shoulder. I swung the mug, which was in my right hand, full force into his face. He went down like a ton of bricks. He looked very still, as I must have done when I was hit on the chin with the rifle butt. The barman shouted to me and pointed to the door behind him. I shot round the counter through two rooms and out the back door. Then it hit me. The second room I had passed through was the kitchen and there on the table was half a loaf of homemade bread. So, I shot back in again, whipped it off the table and was gone.

Now, because I'd made my exit from this bar by the opposite way to my entry, for all purposes I was lost. There was no time to hang around because it was obvious someone had called that policeman and there would be hell to pay in a very short time. Then once more my luck came good. As I turned from a side street a man's voice said, "Follow me, but not too close."

At that, he walked off with me following some 20 yards behind him. The pace was quite brisk. I didn't realise that the village could have so many turnings and streets. We then came to a hill with small houses on either side. Three-quarters of the way up he stopped, opened a plain wooden door at the side of the house, which was positioned almost on the pavement, entered and left it ajar. I followed.

I thought to myself, if I had to get back to that vino bar it would take me a week. We entered the house from the yard and to my surprise there were about 20 people inside. Three of them spoke perfect English and were very well dressed. There were three women around the age of 30 years, one of whom spoke a fair amount of English. I rather fancied this one at the time, she was very pretty and it passed through my mind that I must be recovering my old self. They all seemed to think that I looked very comical, as they burst out laughing when I walked in, and all seemed to be asking the same question of the chappie who had led me there.

"Where did you find this one?" seemed to be the question.

The young woman, who spoke some English, came over smiling and took from underneath my arm the half loaf of bread. I had forgotten about it completely. I suppose I did look a bit odd, so I just laughed with them and that made me feel very good.

I was told that they were here for the sole purpose of helping escaped POWs and they asked me for my name, rank and number. I thought maybe they hoped to be paid off at the end of the war. I had a nice hot bath, the first since I was near Rome. I was given a complete change of clothing, which included a good jacket, a smashing meal with vegetables and a very comfortable warm bed. It was about 2 p.m. when I took my bath and had my meal. I couldn't resist trying out the bed.

The next thing I knew it was 10 a.m. the next day. I got up, slipped on my trousers and left the bedroom, more out of curiosity than anything else. I heard voices and movement from behind one of the doors, which I thought I had remembered as being the kitchen. I opened it and it was, but this time it was being used as an operating theatre. An operation was being performed on the kitchen table. It turned out that one of the French prisoners they were helping to put on the road for home had gone down with an acute appendicitis. By the time I left he was well on the road to recovery. I had been in the house for three days when I discovered that Italy had declared war on the Germans. I found this difficult to understand, as most of Italy, from what I could gather, was occupied by Germans. I couldn't see how this could help, but it did.

I was in the house for six days and feeling on top of the world, and didn't feel like moving off. But I was told that, in the morning after first light, I would be leaving with a guide who would take me to where I would be transported by truck, to a partisan hideout, on the side of a mountain called Montagnola.

I was called early and given a large plate of stew for breakfast, which, in the circumstances, tasted delicious. It was time to move. I had clear instructions on what to do. I was once more to follow the guide, 20 to 30 paces behind him, and would be told what to do when we arrived at the trucks.

We left the house and the road was dead empty and very quiet. It was quite a fresh morning. I followed behind the guide and for the second time my attention was drawn to my brogues and their army pattern. The noise the studs were making on the footpath was terrific. Everything was so quiet apart from my boots drumming away. The guide looked over his shoulder at my boots, then at me. He just shrugged his shoulders and we continued on. We made yet another detour and once more I thought I could never find my way back to that house. The circuitous route was deliberate, as they didn't want anyone to know exactly where the house was situated. That certainly made sense.

We walked some 20 minutes and passed the odd civilian on his cycle going about his business. By now we were somewhere on the edge of the village. We entered a yard filled with barrels. There stood an open truck with barrels already loaded. They were large and standing upright.

The lid was lifted from one of the barrels near the front end of the vehicle and I was told to get in. My instructions were not to lift the lid at any time and if the truck stopped I shouldn't even breathe. I knew what they wanted. The truck could well be stopped, as indeed it was, and any movement could have brought down the lot of us. I imagined that most of the barrels might have an occupant in each but as it turned out I was wrong. There was only one other, an ex-Italian army major, who was going to make his way south to join the army. I hadn't any idea what that meant. I felt he must have been OK; otherwise he would not have been mixed up with this lot. The journey at the beginning was smooth enough, but after what seemed ages I got very stiff and felt like standing up. We then must have struck a rough road for the barrel seemed to be banging against those around it. At least it helped my stiffness. I am sure if the barrel had been on the outer edge of the truck it and me would have finished up in the ditch. The truck slowed down and came to a halt. I heard voices. They were German.

I heard the driver talking away in a loud voice and in a very friendly manner. I also heard what sounded like a gate opening. The truck moved on for a matter of minutes, and then stopped again. The hooter on the truck was sounded and there were more German voices. There was clattering and thumping on the truck. I thought, oh dear, they are unloading it.

This went on for some ten minutes. Then we moved off again. It turned out that this truck delivered two of these barrels of vino twice weekly, to a small German HQ. We had actually been in and out. I thought "Blimey they have a nerve."

Chapter 15

A PENKNIFE AND A PIECE OF STRING

We arrived at the partisan hideout. The journey had taken about one and half to two hours. The so-called hideout was nothing more than a farm on the side of the hill. There seemed to be only one road in and out.

The lid was lifted and to my horror I found I couldn't get out. I couldn't even move. I had stiffened up too much to do anything. They all thought this was a big giggle. Two of them caught me under the armpits and hoisted me out. It was agony.

In this mountain hideout I was the lone Englishman, amongst a mixture of Yugoslavs and Italians. The food was out of this world, more meat than one could eat. It was all a bit overwhelming. They all seemed to have their own business to attend to and at times I wondered what I was doing there.

The Yugoslavs were certainly active every night. They went off on their individual raids, armed to the teeth. What they got up to, I didn't bother to find out. I couldn't stick it any longer, I was getting nowhere fast, and so I left.

I scrounged a loose canvas rucksack, ample food, a penknife and a length of string. I remembered my father once telling me, if you have a penknife, a piece of string and a pound note in your pocket, you couldn't want. I didn't have a pound note but I had some lire.

I had now been free for some 25 days and I had gotten nowhere. I would have given my back teeth for a map but none of the partisans seemed interested in helping me. But, I thought at the time, why should they, I was of little use to them.

It was the end of October, give or take a couple of days, when I left. I said nothing, for it was of little good, and once more made my way south.

A main road on my left seemed to run southwards. I thought if I walked in the hills, I would just about see this road and would be comparatively safe. There certainly was quite a lot of military traffic on it.

I had been walking for five days, sleeping in woods each evening and covering some eight to ten miles per day. I shall never forget those hills. They were soul destroying and being across country made it even worse. My food, which consisted mostly of bread and cheese, was now down to my last evening's chew and I wished now that I had rationed my cigarettes. I was gasping for a drag.

Farmhouses with a few outbuildings were scattered around and the odd village, small and large, could be seen but I was hesitant to enter any of these again.

I settled for the night and thought, 'Five days. God, how many more?' And was feeling very depressed. I then thought of those who had not escaped and wondered what they might be doing. At least I was free and that made me a feel a thousand times better. I thought, as I was sitting there, that I needed to keep some record of the days I had been walking as I felt I would forget the number quite easily if it mounted up.

The following morning I cut from a bush a short piece of twig about half an inch thick. I grinned to myself for I had done that before to make the dice. I removed the bark and cut five notches for the five days I had already walked, and would record another notch each evening. I put the knife and stick into my pocket and moved off.

Two days later I still had not eaten, but I was used to it. Food would have been very nice but it was better not to think about it. It was during the afternoon, I was walking along a track and there in front of me, on a bend, appeared, at first sight to be, Count Dracula himself. Count Dracula had always impressed me when I was a boy, and I am quite sincere when I say that this was my first reaction. It was in fact a priest. As he passed he said, "Good day, where are you going?"

I took a chance and said, "I am going south. I am English."

With an amount of sign language and the smattering of Italian I had picked up, it was agreed that I should follow him. We walked for a short distance to a farm, or what one might call a smallholding.

A brief conversation went on between the farmer and the priest, whom I noticed for the first time, seemed quietly spoken. I was asked to stay in one of the small outbuildings, which held minor farm machinery and general rubbish. The priest returned that evening and I was asked into the house. It seemed as if the whole family had gathered to see me but I realised afterwards that in actual fact it was the priest's presence that had drawn them there.

There, running down the centre of the room was a large plain wooden table, scrubbed beautifully bare. It was some ten feet long and three feet wide. On one side was a long bench and along the other, chairs. Over a large black kitchen range stood a rather large black pot and simmering beside it another pot that was exuding all sorts of fantastic smells, which to a hungry man was a bit much—I only hoped I was going to help eat whatever was cooking. I need not have worried. I was

Ben's escape route, Map of Italy: A rough guide.
"He said we were some two hours' walk from Foligno."

invited to sit on the left of the farmer, who was seated at the head of the table. The priest sat on his right.

Before sitting down, the large pot was brought to the table and the contents were gently poured all over it. The contents were like thick batter. There was an art in what they were doing. The layer on the table finished up a good half an inch thick and none was spilt. The small pot was brought. This contained small pieces of meat, (small wild birds) and loads of tomato puree. This was once more gently poured over the top and then spread all over the base with a long flat thin piece of scrubbed wood. They called it 'polenta'.

The whole table was surrounded by the family from near and far. It was the farmer's wedding anniversary. What a wedding anniversary this would be for him if Jerry walked in to find me there. I looked at the priest and pointed to the door.

"Tedesci?" (Germans), I said.

The rest of the family looked at me with some concern. The priest shook his head, "No, not tonight."

We were about to start eating when a thought struck me.

"Let us make a Carta Geographical un Italia." I suggested.

They went mad. They thought it was a fantastic idea. The farmer got up and with the handle of his spoon cut out the outline of Italy and finished where I was sitting at the toe. He then gave instructions for all to eat to the line only and then stop. Well, that was all right for those seated from three-quarters of the way up down to our end, but for those at the top it wasn't so good. If you have in your mind the shape of Italy you will understand why.

The farmer cut away at the foot to arrive at Taranto. The priest was busy going round the heel and I was shaping up past the toe to the leg nicely. Then there was a scream from the other end of the table. One of the nippers couldn't stick it any

117

longer; he had scooped his spoon right into the top end. There was absolute hell to pay. The old man got up and screamed at him and so did most of the others at the table. I kept eating and the priest just kept shrugging his shoulders and spreading out his hands. I felt sure I would never have another evening like this one. It was smashing.

The map was cut. I asked the priest where we were. He said that we were some two hours walk from a town called Foligno and there were quite a number of Germans there. I asked him where the Allies were. He drew a line across the table and pointed to one side, Rome and to the other, Pescara, about one hundred miles from where we were. The farmer suggested that I should stay with them until the Allies arrived. He said that the arrival would not be far off. I thanked them very sincerely and said I would leave the next day.

Having eaten well and having had a good scrub up and shave with the farmer's razor, I was itching to get home. It turned out it was a good thing I did leave, as our troops were nowhere near the Rome–Pescara line.

By first light the priest returned with a small Beretta pistol and a map of rather small scale, but of great use. The Beretta was a mistake. I should never have taken it as it proved later.

He asked me to wait for two hours because a young man he knew wanted to join me. He would be travelling south to join the Italian Army and help the Allies fight the Germans.

"Blimey," I thought to myself.

"He is doing well, fighting on both sides in one war. And he's the second one I've encountered."

My new companion arrived. Apparently he had been commissioned in the Italian Army, prior to defeat. He was some 30 years of age.

The priest gave him loads of information about the Germans

and said we were to pass on the east side of Foligno. I didn't know how I was going to feel about this chap. I had a feeling I was going to lose some of my independence, but I thought I would give it a go. I was free to leave him at any time I wanted and I had the map, which was rather important to me.

As it turned out he was a smashing chap, very keen and much too fast a walker for me. He was very much fitter than I was. However, he reduced his speed to what I set for myself. He was able to approach a farmhouse, find out what reaction he got and if favourable, we would stay the night in the outbuildings and very often be supplied with bread and sometimes soup. Rather more importantly, he was in the position of being able to ask so many questions about the German positions. This was most useful, for on many occasions we would have walked straight into them, especially as we neared their front lines.

It was getting very cold. And the higher one walked up these hills, the colder it became. When we bypassed Aquila, the Gran Sasso (the highest peak in the Apennines) had plenty of snow on it. Our latest information was that the Allies were some 20 to 30 miles ahead, which made the next two days walking easy.

There were still no Allies, just Germans.

We felt that the next day we would meet up with somebody and we did; a German patrol of seven men, all carrying light automatic weapons.

Chapter 16

TAKEN AS A SPY

The area was wooded and we were walking round the curve of the wood. We could not see more than 50 yards ahead. I felt afterwards it could have been my fault, as at the sight of that lot, I just panicked and dove straight into what undergrowth there was beside me and lay quiet. Within seconds Jerry was there.

"Come here! Come here!" they shouted.

I glanced up slowly and I must have looked a proper clot. I wasn't even properly concealed. The Italian had just stood still. By now he was talking rapidly in Italian to the sergeant in charge of the patrol, as if trying to talk his way out of it. He was searched and they found nothing. I was searched. They found the Beretta pistol and my pamphlet from the Pope quoting "God Save the King". It was in a way rather interesting. The sergeant didn't seem concerned about the pistol. All he could do was look at the pamphlet and keep repeating "God Save the King" in the most peculiar accent. He stopped and looked me in the eyes and said with a smile,

"Englander."

What could I say but "Yes."

We walked on with them until we came to a small village on the side of the hill. They took the first donkey they saw from a farm type building within the village and made my Italian friend load some sacks of potatoes onto its back. I went to give him a hand but was pushed back by one of the patrol. The sergeant gave me a cigarette—Italian make. He lit it for me and I nearly brought up with coughing; it was so long since I had had a smoke.

I offered the cigarette to my Italian friend, but was told, "No!" by the Jerry. It was obvious that they had no time for the Italians who had turned against them.

We were taken back to Agnone, the town that we had bypassed no more than an hour before. It had received a fair amount of shelling. We were put on a small 15-hundredweight type truck and taken along the main road going east from Agnone for some four of five miles, where we drove into a large wood with a type of lodge house and many tents. This turned out to be Jerry's HQ for this sector. This is where Jerry made his first mistake—taking me in there and driving us from Agnone in an open vehicle, without blindfolds.

We remained in the truck for some 20 minutes. I was then taken into the main building by the biggest fella I have ever seen—he must have stood six and half to seven feet tall. I had to look up at him and I'm six feet.

We came to a door and the German soldier knocked. It was opened by a ferret-faced little Jerry, who must have been a clerk. We were expected, that was for sure. The big Jerry gave me a push.

The room was quite large. At the other side, sitting behind a desk, was a rather smart, well-dressed German officer. I instinctively saluted. I couldn't help it for it was quite automatic. He looked right. The salute was appreciated and he smiled, "Now Tommy, what are you doing in our lines?"

Before I could think of an answer he asked another question. "Where is your home town?"

"I live near Colchester, in Essex." I replied.

"I know that place well, I have spent a lot of time in Chelmsford," he said.

I realised he was genuine as he could not have thought that one out so quickly. I looked straight at him, and thought that he must be some 40 years of age. I couldn't help but think that he had a pleasant and kind face.

"Now tell me what you have been up to over the past few weeks?"

I didn't reply.

"Who helped you along your journey?'

I couldn't have answered that if I had wanted to because I didn't know.

"I don't know." I said.

"Come, come, you look to me as if you have been travelling for quite a long time, or are you just working behind our lines?"

"NO!" I replied firmly, for I knew the answer to that was true.

"I am an escaped prisoner of war and I'm only doing what any prisoner would do, given the chance."

He looked at me again with that friendly smile. The smile disappeared and a stern expression came over his face. He looked straight at me.

"You will be shot tomorrow and I will give you the details. You will be taken back behind our lines with a lot of other rabble we have here. You will then be shot in whatever town the firing party chooses. Do you understand?"

"Yes," I replied. "But you can't do that. I am covered by the

Geneva Convention as a POW."

He then appeared to lose his temper a little. He raised his voice: "There is nothing in the Geneva Convention to say that you can walk behind our lines in civilian clothes, armed and with no identification."

He rattled an order to the big Jerry beside me and I was pushed towards the door, which the clerk was holding open. The officer then spoke in German and English simultaneously.

The guard stopped me.

"Tommy, just think you were only eight miles from freedom. If you had travelled by the west side of Agnone and not by the east, you would have stood a much better chance. We haven't many troops on that side." That was Jerry's second mistake.

We left.

Chapter 17

TO BE SHOT!

I was pushed through a low window into a bare room. The room had one door, which was locked up and I thought, "This seems strange."

The window opening consisted of a frame only, no sashes, nothing. An armed guard was positioned outside. I was now alone and had time to think. And that wasn't good. For 53 days I had been free and many times cold, wet and miserable and now this goon says I'm to be shot. To make it worse there didn't seem to be much I could do about it.

Within the hour the Italian, I had travelled with, was pushed through the window. Jerry has also ordered him to be shot. Then in came two Arabs. That surprised me. Apparently they had been with the South African Army, they had tacked themselves on as servants. How they got into this situation I didn't bother to ask. To be quite truthful I didn't even like talking.

Darkness had fallen and a greater depression came over me. I felt I had no chance of surviving this one. I must have dropped off to sleep for I was awoken by voices and movement. Somebody else was coming through the window.

It turned out to be a British Army officer, in uniform. This I discovered at first light.

The officer was younger than myself and looked a little shaken. He told me that he had been taken prisoner that morning during an attack across a river. It was quite obvious that he would be OK and would be treated as a POW. We talked and I told him my position. I gave him my parents' home address and asked him to contact them after the war and explain to them what had happened. I felt much better having done that.

He was confident that they would not carry out the execution. By now we had in the room five Italian civilians who had been helping POWs, (I didn't fancy their chances much), the Italian officer I had been travelling with, the two Arabs, the English officer and myself.

It was around 11 o'clock when the guard stuck his head in the window and ordered out the Italians and the two Arabs. This left the English officer and myself. He looked at me as much as to say, there you are, what did I tell you. Ten minutes passed and I was just relaxing when the guard stuck his head and shoulders through the window and said, "Englander! Come!" at the same time as pointing his finger at me.

Two five-ton trucks covered with canvas hoods stood outside. I was pushed into the last one. Inside was the officer I had travelled with, the two Arabs and an armed German soldier. There was also loads of loot up the front in the form of sheepskins and potatoes. The guard ordered me to the front of the truck and indicated that he wanted me to sit down and keep quiet.

We moved off. It was around noon. We were travelling northwards.

The Italian whispered in my ear, "Escapo?"

I shrugged my shoulders to indicate that I couldn't see how. He whispered something else and for the first time he made me ratty. I did not want to talk. I felt I had to think. I glared at him to show my disapproval and moved slightly away. The guard who was squatting at the front turned immediately pointing his light automatic at us and at the same time shouted something in German, which obviously meant, "Keep still!"

I lay back on the sheepskins when a voice within me said, "Get to the back of the truck. Get to the back of the truck."

I am not an overly religious man and had not experienced anything quite like this before. It felt strongly spiritual and, whether or not it was, it continued for what seemed an age but could only have been minutes.

I shouted to the guard to draw his attention, for what reason I knew not. He looked at me and instinctively, by the movement of my hand and mouth, I indicated that I wanted to be sick. He pointed his light machine gun directly at me and beckoned me to the rear of the truck. I hung over the tailboard as if in a very bad way.

Then it happened. The truck stopped so suddenly. It threw us all over the place. There was a lot of shouting from the front of the cab in German. It all happened so quickly. The Jerry jumped out, followed by me—we were being attacked by two British fighter-bombers.

I ran into the field by the roadside. It was terrible. The scream of the aircraft and the hail of cannon shells and bullets were unbelievable. I threw myself to the ground by which time the aircrafts had passed and were on their way back again, with their guns rattling. The last one of the two dropped a bomb, which fell short of the truck in which I had been. I felt my head swimming and my ears ringing with all the chaos and noise.

As soon as they had passed I was up again and running. It

was only a matter of 30 yards or so before I hit the ground again. Then, to my horror, I noticed that pushing up tight to me was a German—one of the party, but not the one from my truck. I forgot all about the aircraft at the sight of him. I got up and ran on across the fields with an uphill climb all the way.

Chapter 18

THE 23RD PSALM

The next thing I remembered was that it was sometime after midnight and I was lying amongst trees and large rock. I must have passed out with exhaustion. I was very, very cold.

It is difficult to describe the feeling. All seemed very peaceful and I felt so happy, I could well have cried. I leaned against a large boulder and thought about the event which had passed, then fell asleep.

I was awake before dawn, which pleased me for I didn't really know what cover I had. So, as the daylight broke I moved further up the hill and through the wood. There, I was able to sit under some shelter to get my bearings and recover my senses properly. The sun came up behind me. I got up, turned to my left and was on my way.

I had one problem. I really didn't know how far we had travelled in the truck. I had been walking for some two hours when I noticed a woman working the slopes of her smallholding. I walked up to her and she looked frightened.

I said, "I am a German, direct me to Agnone."
She rattled on.

"Slowly," I said.

She pointed to the valley ahead and said it lay beneath the hill beyond. As the crow flies, that would be my route. I estimated it was some three or four miles. I left the woman to get on with her task and walked on.

"Now Mr German," I thought, I must go to the west of Agnone but with more caution than before, so I carefully proceeded down the hill across the valley and up the other side. I could see Agnone slightly over to my left and some three miles off but felt I had travelled far enough for this day for I needed to tackle the passing of Agnone with a fresh mind.

My feet were hurting very badly.

I had not taken my boots off for weeks and I was afraid to, because the last time I did I could hardly get them on again. The effort of trying had been extremely painful. So, I sat in a spinney for the rest of the afternoon and night, once more freezing cold.

By the time morning came I was surrounded by thick mist. This properly upset my well-laid plans for an early start. By 10 a.m. it had practically cleared. If I had been on lower ground I would not have had the mist at all but I didn't know that at the time. Within two hours I had arrived at the main road, running west out of Agnone. I crossed it with no trouble but, at the same time, I used considerable caution.

I continued my journey for a further two hours and then once more decided to stop for the rest of the day. I had travelled some five miles that day and felt that was chancing enough. At least I was now past Agnone. As I lay back in the wood that night I started to become very excited at the thought of being nearly home; forgetting the fact, of course, that I was still a long boat ride from the UK. I realised that, yet again, I had not eaten for some four days. One could sometimes grin about that sort of thing. It became routine.

The next day I walked for six hours, and used great caution covering some five or six miles only. I felt I must now be near the British lines because during my journey I could clearly hear the gunfire of both sides. Yet, somehow, I thought it seemed a quiet war. I suppose it could be like that at times.

I felt rather tired so once more decided that I would stop for the night. There, no more than two hundred yards away was a farm. Oh, how I would have liked to spend the night in there.

"No chance," I thought, "But I will try one of the outbuildings at dusk."

I ended up sharing an old shed with a cow; there was ample straw around. The farmer must have hidden him in there to stop Jerry taking him away for slaughter. I settled myself to one side of the old cow where there was the most straw. By now I had got beyond thinking. The straw was warm and I had shelter so I was soon asleep.

This night I had fantastic dreams of when I was young, rolling in the stream that ran through the field below my home. I was all wet and warm. All was laughter and happiness. Then I woke up. The old cow had moved her arse round and pissed all over me whilst I slept. There was not much I could do about this. I just moved forward to the eating end and settled down again.

It was daylight when I awoke again. I wondered how I was going to get out of this lot without being seen. Not only was I wet and had cow shit all over my trouser legs, being seen would mean the risk of being re-captured, something I couldn't bear at this late stage. With trepidation, I eased open the door which grated on the ground, as it had when I had entered. There standing within a foot of me was the farmer.

He looked at me and crossed himself twice. "What in God's

name?" he must have thought to himself.

I didn't hesitate, "Where are the British and Italian Allies?" I asked.

I thought it better to include his side as we were still in German occupied territory. He pointed to a small river, which was part of the Trigno. He informed me that this was no-man's land. I had to agree with him there, in more ways than one.

It was dangerous to cross the river because it was patrolled by German troops who had the habit of shooting at any movement on the river. I asked him how deep the river was and he shrugged, held his hand outstretched above his head, then down to his waist, then to his knees.

OK. I understood it was all a question of where to cross, so I hesitated for a moment and then proceeded to the river. By the time I had covered 500 yards I was there. The farmer had said, once I crossed this river I was safe behind the British lines. Now for the first time I was really frightened. I really felt as if I'd had it—all the journeying for nothing. I was literally sick with fear. Then a strange feeling came over me and at the same time the voice within me spoke again, not with haste, but with gentleness. The voice was speaking lines from the 23rd Psalm:

"Though, I walk through the valley of the shadow of death, I will fear no evil. For thou art with me."

The voice kept repeating these lines, over and over again.

I entered the river and waded across feeling very strong and free from all cares. I arrived on the other bank and the voice stopped.

It proved to be a very moving and strange experience for me, for I lay on the bank and cried. Really, I suppose, because I was so weak from travelling.

Chapter 19

A FRIENDLY FACE

Now, to find the British. I walked on. Then I couldn't believe it. The Allies and the Germans decided to shoot it out. They were hurling shells at each other and there I was in the middle. This suited me very nicely for as long as none fell short I would be OK. The barrage lasted some half an hour.

I was on my way again. I came to a very small village and the first person I saw was a soldier whom I thought at first was British. I called out to him. He turned, lifted his light machine gun and pointed it in my direction. I put my hands up. I didn't want to get shot at this stage. By this time four or five others had appeared. I saw then that they were Canadians. They were on patrol. I said a silly thing, "Thanks for the Red Cross parcels."

It was the first thing that came into my head.

"Where the bloody hell have you come from?" the corporal asked.

"I'm an escaped POW," I replied.

"Poor sod," said another.

"We have had several POWs through us over the past weeks,

but never one like you. How long have you been on this trip?"

I thought for a moment, "58 days," I said.

I was given a cigarette and we moved off.

"Jesus," one of them said, "You stink."

"You should have smelt me before I crossed the river." I replied.

I told the corporal that it was most important that I should talk to Battalion HQ before doing anything else.

"I will have to take you to Company HQ first. They will send you over to Batt' HQ," he replied.

We arrived at Company HQ and I was taken by truck to Batt' HQ. I told my story as briefly as possible in respect of the German HQ outside of Agnone. The Battalion Intelligence Officer came in, armed with large-scale survey maps. I was able to point out to him the German position in the wood. It appeared that they had thought it to be in the church in Agnone itself. They were delighted.

"I doubt whether there will be little left of that by morning," said the rather amused Intelligence Captain.

"Now we will have to see what we can do about you."

I was taken back by road to a place called Campobasso, where I seemed to be quite popular. I was treated to a hot bath, a shave and a complete new uniform.

It wasn't until I was getting undressed to bathe that I realised how bad my feet really were. They looked rotten and hurt like hell; the tops of the toes and heels were red raw. I don't know how I stood the pain as I stepped into the bath. It took me over an hour to wash and dress, but I found I couldn't get my socks on, let alone the boots they had given me. Although there was no need, a terror came over me. Because of my lack of freedom to walk properly, I felt as if I might be a prisoner again. I felt a cold sweat coming off my forehead.

On leaving the bathroom I realised that I was in the officers' quarters. One of the 'other rank' staff came up and said dinner would be ready in half an hour.

"Where am I?" I asked.

"In the officers' quarters," he replied.

"Look here," I said, "I am only a Corporal, somebody has made a mistake."

"No they haven't," he replied. "They want to question you during dinner."

I drew his attention to my bare feet. "I can't get my socks or boots on. I can't go in like this."

"I wouldn't worry if I were you, they won't." He replied.

I entered what was the dining room. It was nice, considering it was up front. There were a couple of officers already there. They looked at me as if they'd had a hard day. They were very friendly and I was given a large bottle of Canadian beer.

Eight of us in all sat down to dinner and that was the first, and only, time I was waited on during my tour of service. During dinner I was asked about the journey and the various movements of troops and columns of vehicles I had seen. One of the officers kept making notes. He seemed most keen about the HQ in the wood outside Agnone. By and large the hour and a half that I was in there was very enjoyable.

One of the officers said that the Medical Officer would visit me that evening in my room to have a look at my feet.

I returned to a room and bed for the night when the M.O. came in. He looked at my poor old feet, dressed and lightly bandaged them and gave me an injection.

I woke with a cup of tea at about 10 a.m., got up and was given a late breakfast of fried corned beef, which was fantastic. At 12 noon, the Intelligence Officer contacted me to say that the German HQ in the wood outside Agnone no longer existed. It had been flattened by shellfire. He thanked me for the information.

I was grinning to myself as I left the Canadians by truck for Bari. I was thinking of the German Officer who had condemned me to death. I felt somehow he would never see Chelmsford again, but I might. At the same time I was hoping that the English Officer had been moved.

I arrived in Bari to a type of transit camp run by the British. I had a large envelope addressed to the Officer Commanding, which I was to hand in. The driver stopped and spoke to the sergeant, asking him where we should report. He told the sergeant I was an escaped POW. The sergeant looked across at me and said, "Where the bloody hell have you been? We cleared all the POWs weeks ago. Escaped, I'll be buggered. The Itis left and you all walked out."

This could have been the case for those that were further south.

My uniform had no insignia of rank and he naturally thought I was a buck private. He told the driver where he could spend the night and told me to get out of the truck and follow him. I must admit I looked rather comical. Over my bandaged feet I was wearing two pairs of thick grey army socks and my boots were slung over my shoulder. The truck moved off and there I stood.

"Put your bloody boots on," he said.

"I can't." I replied. "My feet are sore and stop throwing your fucking weight about and take me to my billet."

"Look here my good friend," he said sarcastically,

"Anymore talk and you will be straight inside again. Then you will have something to think about."

I could have killed the bastard. I started to wonder what I

135

had come to. I spent the night once more in a double tier bunk in a temporary building.

The next morning I overslept and missed my breakfast. I was awoken by a lance corporal and told that I had to be at the RSMs office right away. I dressed, had a quick rinse and followed the lance corporal, still with my boots under my arm and no hat. The carrying of my boots must have been instinct from training received from my POW days. I thought someone might nick them.

I was shown into a room where a captain was seated. Apparently he had conducted all the interviews of many POWs who had passed through.

"Sit down", he said. "Now let's start, they opened the gates and you walked out. Now, let's carry on from there shall we?"

I was livid. There was nothing I could say or do to get my own back, so I didn't reply.

The captain looked up at me, paused, then said, "And then what happened?"

"Nothing, I just walked home as you might say."

The door opened, a young officer came in with the envelope I had brought from the Canadians. It had been opened. The sergeant to whom I gave it must have handed it in to the Office, as it was addressed to the C.O.

I was surprised when he took out a single letter as it was much more bulky than that when I had it. The captain read whatever was in the letter and looked up at me with a smile.

"Forget my initial question Corporal and let's start again. Do you smoke?"

"Yes, Sir," I replied.

He pushed across the table a round tin of Players. I took one and he gave me a light. "I see by this letter that you were

136

popular with the Canadians."

"They were very friendly, much more than I can say about the sergeant I met last night." I replied.

"Right," said the captain, "I want the full story from beginning to end and I don't care how long it takes."

I told him what had happened; leaving out those parts that I thought were irrelevant. When I had finished he looked at me and said, "I don't think I would have believed you if I hadn't interviewed the two Arabs three days ago."

"Blimey," I thought.

"They did well."

I asked where they were now. He said they had been sent to a displaced persons camp for shipment to Egypt. I asked the officer what my chances were for a bit of leave in the UK. He informed me that I would be shipped home as soon as the War Office had confirmed that I was the person I claimed to be. I found this difficult to understand and told him so. This was the system and no one could break it.

"And, anyway", he said, "How do we know that you are not a German spy?"

At least he grinned at his own remark.

I felt a bit fed up with this lot. The War Office could take ages to confirm my particulars. Somehow I must get away from here.

Chapter 20

SHENANIGANS

That evening I went over to the NAAFI (Navy, Army Airforce Institute), where I met two Americans who were staying overnight. I got talking to them and after a few beers (which they had bought me, for I had no money of my own) they suggested that I should travel with them to the port of Taranto the next day. They had the idea of my hitching a ride across the Mediterranean on one of their boats and then hitch from Algiers to the UK by plane. According to them it would be easy.

The next day I left, without ceremony, with the two Yanks by truck to Taranto. The run didn't take more than an hour and a half.

Oh dear! I found the Yanks more helpful than the Canadians and that was saying something. Within two hours I was aboard a big American Landing Craft. I hadn't even seen anything like this before. I had been given a big American fur lined flying jacket to keep me warm. This was super. Naturally I was the only Englishman on board and I was made very welcome.

We landed in North Africa, but instead of it being Algiers

it was Bizerte. I now had to get to Algiers, four hundred plus miles away.

I followed all those who were in transit and finished up in an American transit camp. Here I had all the help and advice I could ask for. The Yanks said they would put me on a train for Algiers and supply me with enough blankets, which I could sell to the Arabs on route to make some money for the odd beer, or two.

My feet by this time were very much improved. I had discarded my British Army hob-nailed boots in Taranto for a handful of lire and had been given a nice pair of suede desert boots. The crepe soles were a great improvement. I felt I would never ever have got those hard, new leather ones on.

The train turned out to be once more cattle trucks, but this time unlocked. I also had two Yankees to keep me company and we had loads of food and beer. I also had four blankets.

"Gee," said one of the Yanks, "Why didn't you bring more? You can't sell those. You will need them, however don't worry, leave it to us."

During the journey, one blanket was sold at least a dozen times but we did lose a single one. The system was that whenever the train stopped, wherever it was along the route, North Africans would appear as if from nowhere. The deal would be struck at the last moment then, just as the train was moving off, the money and blanket would be exchanged. As soon as the money was in the hand, the blanket would be yanked back from the unsuspecting Arab. At one stop they must have experienced this previously, because they yanked the blanket first and kept the money. That was one thing, you could never really trust any of the North African tribes!

We arrived in Algiers but the hope of getting a flight home was out of the question. It had been done a lot in the past. I gathered that some would go home for the weekend only and then return. Now that little game had been stopped.

I hitched a lift to the racecourse where, I learned, there was a large British transit camp. I moved in and could have stayed there if I had wanted to until the end of the war. The only difference would be I would never be able to draw money.

I went to the transit office and made myself known, and I can tell you I wasn't popular! I made the mistake of telling them about being in Bari, and how I'd chosen not to hang around. They didn't want to excuse the fact that I'd left without notice. So, to tide me over, they somewhat begrudgingly gave me the equivalent of one pound in pay. This would be deducted from my official pay when the confirmation that proved my identity was received from the War Office and the Pay Master General's Office.

It wasn't much good being in Algiers with a pound, not even in those days. However, I did have quite a number of francs that the Americans had acquired from me selling blankets.

In Algiers, the Americans couldn't get into the better class brothels in their Yankee uniforms because the girls thought that they were rampant with VD. So it was quite easy to make a quick buck by changing uniforms with the Yanks down an alley and then waiting for them to come out of the brothel and change back again.

For many, life in this transit camp was an anxious waiting game of day in, day out. With everyone so desperate to get home and not really knowing when that might be, the embarkation list for the UK was closely watched by most. Though I didn't feel it necessary for me, as I had only been there a few days, I did, however, check it and to my surprise and delight, my name was up for transit the following day. I couldn't understand how that came about. I felt sure they had not heard from the War Office. However, I boarded the next day and was sailing home to see Ena and my family.

Chapter 21

HOME TO ENA

On arrival in the UK, I was taken to Croydon with many others. Accommodation was a requisitioned house. With double tier bunks it was an improvement indeed. My room had four of these bunks and I had the top one for myself. The first day there I was given a pay book and a week's money. It was not until then that I discovered I was a sergeant. I had been promoted before capture without confirmation. The same night it was decided, amongst the eight of us in the room, to go out on the beer. This we did and I personally got 'blotto'.

I awoke the next morning not knowing where I was and totally confused. My eyes and nose felt full of dust, I was alone in the room and felt as if I was weighted down. This was my first reaction. My second was panic. As I looked up I could see daylight. During the night a number of bombs had fallen in the road. Prior to this the warning had gone and our home had been evacuated. According to my buddies who shared the room with me, they had shaken and called me. I must have gone to sleep again for I had no memory of this. There I was with plaster and bits of batten all over my bunk. The whole room was a shambles. Thank God, I thought, we didn't get a direct hit. I shook my clothes off, got dressed and went outside.

I reported to HQ, which was situated in a large house. From stores I was issued with a new battle dress and told that I had to attend parade within the hour. We were going as 'extras' in a film that they were making about General Montgomery.

British General Bernard Law Montgomery was even more famous. With soaring popularity his nickname, 'Monty', was on the lips of every British person. From the outset 'Monty' had recognised the importance of his public persona and how he could successfully use it to build morale and promote himself as a leader of men. Montgomery was promoted to Field Marshal on September 1st, 1944.

We were taken by truck to a large park and there we waited for hours until the General arrived. He stood on a large staging arrangement. On a given signal, we all rushed forward, waving our hands in the air and shouting with jubilation. Personally, I hadn't had any breakfast and it looked as if we might miss dinner. I also hadn't been on leave yet.

Within a matter of days I was given a fortnight's leave and was told that my posting orders would be sent to me.

After a few weeks on returning to my unit in Wales I was sent to an officer's training unit, having passed a selection board. Whilst on this course I was given three days leave to attend Buckingham Palace for a decoration—I was to receive the Military Medal, (MM).

I arrived at Buckingham Palace with my father and Ena. Here we were separated. I was taken to a large room with big columns; very plush with everything one would expect to find in a palace. Congregated in this room were a large number of people: Naval officers with loads of gold braid, Air Force types, and Army senior officers with their red tabs. I must admit I felt quite inferior with my two little pieces of white tape slipped on my epaulettes. It wasn't easy moving amongst this lot.

In those days, you couldn't even say, "Excuse me," and push past braid. I did, however, find a sergeant who looked just as much out of place as I did, so I introduced myself. At this time I had no insignia of rank on my sleeves, just my white tabs denoting officer cadet.

MANNINGTREE MAN'S MILITARY MEDAL

Twice Escaped From Germans In Italy

The award of the Military Medal to Corporal E. F. (Ben) Reynolds, of Manningtree, for "gallant and distinguished service in the face of the enemy" marks another stage in this soldier's fighting career.

Corporal Reynolds, who is the younger son of C.P.O. and Mrs. A. E. Reynolds, of "Midge," Colchester-road, Lawford, has served overseas for three years, and while serving in Libya was captured by the Germans. He was handed over to the Italians as a prisoner of war and taken to Italy.

In Italy he was held as a prisoner of war for 18 months before being handed over to German control. He succeeded in escaping, however, and spent 38 days on foot in enemy-occupied territory before being recaptured by the Germans.

He escaped a second time and succeeded in reaching the Allied lines, returning home on leave last December.

Press cutting to say that Ben was presented with the Military Medal (MM)

Ten minutes or so had passed when I said to the sergeant, "I feel like a smoke."

"So do I." He replied.

"Do you think we should?" he asked, "Nobody else is smoking."

"Here, have a Woodbine." I said.

The sergeant took the Woodbine and we lit up. Do you know, much to my surprise, within two minutes they were nearly all smoking. I thought to myself, where does one put the ash and more importantly the cigarette end.

That was soon answered for me when in came a very important Palace dignitary.

"Gentlemen! Gentlemen!" he called at the top of his voice.

"If you had been permitted to smoke you would have been given ashtrays. Please stop immediately!"

The reaction was quite amusing. The Gold Braid and Red Tabs just did not know what to do with their unfinished cigarettes. I said to the sergeant, "I bet they would give you a pound each to take them away."

I drew the sergeant's attention to what I was doing and he followed. I just put the cigarette in my trouser pocket and quickly nipped the cloth together. This wasn't difficult wearing ordinary regular soldiers' heavy battle dress.

We were then sorted out by name and type of decoration and I went in to receive my medal and shake the hand of the King. I knew from then on that I would never take life for granted.

The end

King George VI in a formal photo.
The King personally shook the hand of each recipient.
Credit: G. Eric and Edith Matson photograph collection at the
Library of Congress.

POSTSCRIPT

Ben's romance and subsequent marriage to our mother Georgina (Ena) helped Ben to pursue his ambitions. On leaving the army the idea of regimented discipline and following orders must have been alien to him and he now knew, from experience, that having courage and an inventive spirit could take him down a path of self-belief and confidence. After a posting with the army, he decided to live in Nigeria where he worked for the Government helping to rebuild the country's infrastructure. Whilst there, Mum and Dad accumulated some financial capital and, with a young family, returned to England where Dad turned his hand to a small grocery business.

In those early days of the '50s, times were tough and the thought of my father having to deliver customers' groceries to their homes by bicycle—carrying the goodies in the front basket and with bags dangling off the handlebars—amuses me somewhat.

When a supermarket chain opened down the street he knew that it would present serious competition, so he turned his hand to photography. Once just a hobby, it wasn't long before Ben was not only a press photographer but also running a successful business with commercial premises.

He was a man who took calculated risks so that he and his family could financially survive when historically many others did not succeed.

In their mid-40s, Ben and Ena chose to live beside the seaside at Selsey Bill, Sussex. Never being one to sit around he always looked to new challenges and to turn his hand to new ventures. Among other things he fished and sold lobsters, bought a caravan site and successfully rebuilt cars. His 'triumph' was a classic car, the Triumph Vitesse, which he rebuilt from scratch.

It was 1972 when I informed Mum and Dad that I was migrating to Australia and whilst Mum may have anticipated it, Dad was dismayed. "You have a great job here, what can you find in Australia that you don't have here?" he asked.

Of course I knew I would have to justify my decision to him, so I rattled off what I had rehearsed and kept referring to the friendly and honest reputation of the Australian people. This seemed to bring him round.

"Mmm, I know what you mean." He said nodding slowly as though resigned. "The only Australians I've ever met were in the War and yes, they were decent chaps. I really liked them."

Eventually the interest that Selsey Bill held for Ben started to wane and, with two daughters in Australia, he and Ena also decided to emigrate there. This was 1989 and he was 69.

Mum and Dad were both very proud when they took Australian citizenship. They spent the last 15 years of their lives together at Bateau Bay in the Central Coast of NSW. Ben was not idle and successfully built and flew radio controlled model aircraft. He learnt the computer and was self-taught on the guitar and electric organ.

And so it was, that Dad never again let slip his first love. Freedom!

He died in August 2004, aged 84, a month after his beloved wife Ena.

Ben is survived by three children, John, Georgina (Gina) and Penny, four grandchildren, and three great-grandchildren.

MARCH 9, 1945

MISTLEY: Lieut. E. F. Reynolds, M.M., of Manningtree, and Miss Edna Dyer, married at St. Mary's Church.
(Photo by J. F. Cracknell.)

Ena teased Ben saying she would only marry him if he obtained a commission.

ACKNOWLEDGEMENTS

Ben wrote this story in the 1970s and it was his ambition to see it published. Had he been alive he would have wanted to thank many for their support and encouragement. I am sure that his wife, Ena, would have been at the top of his list, followed by the Reynolds family in England and Australia.

In Australia, I would like to thank Publisher, Linda Williams, for her enthusiastic foresight and a friendship shared with Di Newsom. Anthony Donger for his illustrations, John Griffiths for his medal photography, Richard Smith for proofreading everything I typed. Finally I thank my husband, Chas Hyde.

Photographs are referenced from our personal collection and the Public Domain, with credits and added historical notes.

In researching this book I've learnt a lot about the North African Campaign, but I've tried not to digress too far away from Dad's personal story. Hopefully my additions have enhanced Ben's story and may even inspire some readers to explore this part of history more.

DISCLAIMER

I apologise for any errors unwittingly made.

Published in 2015 by New Holland Publishers Pty Ltd
London • Sydney • Auckland

Unit 009, The Chandlery 50 Westminster Bridge Road London SE1 7QY UK
1/66 Gibbes Street Chatswood NSW 2067 Australia
218 Lake Road Northcote Auckland New Zealand

www.newhollandpublishers.com

A record of this book is held at the British Library and the National Library of
Australia.

ISBN 9781742576374

Managing Director: Fiona Schultz
Publisher: Linda Williams
Project Editor: Angela Sutherland
Designer: Andrew Quinlan
Production Director: Olga Dementiev
Printer: Toppan Leefung Printing Ltd

10 9 8 7 6 5 4 3 2 1

Keep up with New Holland Publishers on Facebook
www.facebook.com/NewHollandPublishers